On the Origins of Gender Inequality

Joan Huber

Paradigm Publishers
Boulder • London

Published in the United States by Paradigm Publishers, 3360 Mitchell Lane Suite E, Boulder, Colorado 80301 USA.

Paradigm Publishers is the trade name of Birkenkamp & Company, LLC, Dean Birkenkamp, President and Publisher.

Library of Congress Cataloging-in-Publication Data

Huber, Joan, 1925–
On the origins of gender inequality / Joan Huber.
p. cm.
Includes bibliographical references and index.
ISBN-13: 978-1-59451-361-9
ISBN-10: 1-59451-361-9
1. Sex role. 2. Sex discrimination against women. 3. Breastfeeding.
I. Title.
HQ1075.H83 2007
306.4—dc22

2006035795

Printed and bound in the United States of America on acid-free paper that meets the standards of the American National Standard for Permanence of Paper for Printed Library Materials.

Designed and Typeset in New Baskerville by Straight Creek Bookmakers.

11 10 09 08 07 1 2 3 4 5

For William Form and in memory of Janet Saltzman Chafetz

Contents

Preface

THE IDEAS INVOLVED IN WRITING THIS BOOK were spawned by two events of the late 1960s and early 1970s. The first was the emergence of a new wave of the women's movement that ignited interest in the origin of gender inequality. The second event was personal: I adopted the first edition of *Human Societies* for the course in introductory sociology I taught to 503 students each semester at the University of Illinois at Urbana-Champaign. Gerhard Lenski's ecological-evolutionary analysis of human arrangements explained why the technology of food production in a given ecological context (temperature, rainfall, terrain, soil type, and such) shaped the patterns of human organization over time. The theory was based on the fact that we humans, like other living creatures, must eat often or die. The work a given population has to do to get enough to eat profoundly affects the development of its social and economic institutions and the forms of stratification. For example, the use of the plow as chief subsistence tool made peasants, serfs, or slaves of ordinary people, who were considerably worse off both in what they ate and what they did for a living than were their hunter and gatherer ancestors.

However, the theory never explained how it had come to be that women universally were subordinated to men to a greater or lesser degree. For that matter, neither did any other theory then nor does any extant theory to this day address the origin of gender inequality.

Common sense observation indicates that men tend to be bigger and stronger than women and never have had primary responsibility for child care. Men became warriors and leaders. Women stayed with infants and children. But no one explained why these facts made women come in second best. Making the puzzle even harder to solve, most feminists in cultural anthropology and sociology rejected biological data in favor of the view that reality was only a social construction, which precluded serious study of the constraints that pregnancy and lactation set on women's use of time.

A goal of this study is to persuade feminists, both male and female, to include biological data in their studies of social arrangements in order to shed light on the future of gender inequality. Scholars must cope with the fact that the human being is a mammal species that has evolved so as to transcend the limits of all the others. With our big brains and linguistic ability we create cultures and ideologies that interact with our biological heritage to establish the context in which we act and learn what to believe. Moreover, we humans have learned how to alter the social consequences of physiological differences, including those of sex. Human muscles as well as pregnancy and lactation are much the same physiologically as they were thousands of years ago, but technology has altered their social consequences. For example, guns equalize human strength, and population maintenance no longer requires women to be as fruitful as possible. The industrial revolution brought machines to augment muscle power, and since the late 1800s advances in applied science have altered the social consequences of pregnancy and lactation for women living in modern economies. Women's massive entry into the labor force over the past century and their parallel entry into the political arena are in the process of degendering institutions long dominated by men. Trying to explain why the process moved ahead so much over the course of the twentieth century has been interesting, though it will likely continue whether or not anyone develops a theory to explain what is going on.

In the slow gestation of this project, I am indebted to the personnel of the Ohio State Library, a magnificent and helpful organization that made it easy to obtain material from the disciplines in the biological sciences. I am also indebted to the staff of the President's Technology Services: Ken Cherrington, Chris Adams, Elana Costello, Steven Marquart, and Jeff Steucher for trying hard to teach me how to cope with a computer that seemed to change its way of doing things all too often.

I have enjoyed support from academics in various disciplines at other universities. For such encouragement I am duly grateful to Lucia Benaquisto, Rae Lesser Blumberg, Marianne Ferber, Gerhard Lenski, Jane Loeb, Alexandra Maryanski, John Pease, Nancy Rytina, Steven Rytina, and Jonathan Turner. At Ohio State, the group includes Douglas Downey, Clark Larsen, Linda Lobao, Cathy Rakowski, Goldie Shabad, and especially Carole Fink, who helped in more ways than one. Most of all, I am deeply indebted to William Form and the late Janet Saltzman Chafetz for expressing right from the beginning their belief that the project was doable.

Joan Huber

Introduction

LONG TERM RELATIONSHIPS OF SOCIAL INEQUALITY are marked by one pivotal factor: One group has a vested interest in preserving the distribution of resources that the relationship brings (Jackman 1994:7). Men have dominated all human societies; women, none. Claims that asserted the historical existence of human matriarchies erred (Eller 2000). Although the degree of men's control and women's subordination has varied by time and place, gender inequality has always been asymmetrical. Women collectively resemble a pendulum that can swing only to the midpoint of its trajectory. Whether the pendulum will ultimately follow a full trajectory remains uncertain.

The primary purpose of this book is to explain to social scientists and especially to sociologists why the exclusion of biodata from studies of sex and gender stratification has stifled theory and research concerning the universality of women's secondary status. Though gender research continues to thrive in anthropology's biological field (Smuts 1995), few scholars in cultural studies conceptualize human beings as biosocial animals whose evolutionary history could shed light on contemporary patterns of behavior. The use of biodata is also minimal in sociology, though a few researchers have studied the effect of sex hormones on human behavior from a social psychological perspective, as exemplified by the work of Alice Rossi (1994). Others, influenced by Gerhard Lenski's ecological-evolutionary theory (1970), have examined the effects of ecology and technology on social stratification and institutional development. This research has often included a psychological component, as exemplified by the work of Janet Chafetz (1990), Rae Blumberg (1984), and Jonathan Turner (1997).

Yet few of the studies that define humans as biosocial have influenced the study of gender in either sociology or other social sciences. Early in the twentieth century the majority of sociologists and cultural anthropologists rejected biology because they believed that biological research would lead to racism as had happened in French and German anthropology. Many sociologists also feared that biology would invade the turf of a young discipline that was just beginning to define its own area of research. Then in the 1960s, some early primatologists proclaimed that immutable sex differences in physiology ensured that nonhuman primate males would dominate their females, and declared that these findings also applied to humans. In response, the rapidly growing number of women graduate students in cultural anthropology, sociology, and women's studies during the 1970s reinforced the shunning of biology on the grounds that physiological sex differences consigned women to second class citizenship forever. These trends were subsequently enhanced by postmodernist ideas that cast doubt on the entire enterprise of science.

In this book I argue that biological sex differences must be acknowledged if we are to understand why women have always taken so small a part in the activities that bring the most power and prestige. Until early in the twentieth century, women typically were pregnant or lactating during their most vigorous years. That human gestation requires about nine months is well known, but most social scientists have been totally unaware that throughout human history an infant was suckled at intervals of about 15 minutes during the day and less often at night for its first two years, then less often day and night for another two years. The nature of primate milk requires that the infants of chimpanzees, bonobos, and gorillas, and humans be fed almost continuously. Lactation lasts longer in apes, monkeys, and humans than in other mammals of comparable size, and primate mothers have to tote their infants to boot (Hrdy 1999:175). The mode developed among our primate ancestors and persisted among human forager groups because it maximized infant survival. If a forager mother gave birth before her older child could follow along on the daily search for food, the older one died. A forager mother had to carry her infant or park it nearby, for it could not cling to her hairless body with its weak little hands. The mother of an infant bonobo or chimpanzee was coated with hair and her infant's hands were strong. Moreover, the large human brain had come at the cost of a dangerous birth process that produced a relatively undeveloped infant that needed far more care for a longer period of time than did the infant of any other primate mother.

Despite the importance of infant nourishment in reproduction, young children's crucial dependence on human milk has long been ignored due both to problems in collecting data and to male bias (Lancaster 1985:20; Stuart-Macadam 1996:76). Lactation is a topic that is largely absent not only from women's health studies and feminist thought (van Esterik 1989:4) but also from general social science, sociological theory, and (with a few exceptions) from demography. Even feminist Marxists have never been able to resolve the question as to why women became responsible for child care not only under capitalism but also under state socialism (Sokoloff 1980:114, 196).

The rigid constraints of lactation began to loosen about 1900, primarily in modern economies. The extent was not well understood until much later and remains unknown in the social sciences to this day. This book explains why the constraints evolved and persisted for millions of years, why they declined in our species, and what the decline implies for the future of gender equality. Below, I first note earlier efforts to explain male dominance and then briefly examine the historical intertwining of subsistence technology and gender stratification.

Explanations of Male Dominance

For nearly all of human history, the need for humans to be fruitful and multiply was obvious, and male dominance largely went unquestioned during the long period during which no man could feed an infant the only food it could digest. Scientific explanations of gender inequality began to proliferate only in the early 1970s when a new wave of feminism spurred a rise of interest in the universality of women's secondary status. These studies, based primarily on data collected by cultural anthropologists, never really came to a conclusion. For example, sociologist Martin Whyte's (1984:199) comparative study based on a wide range of anthropological data from the Human Relations Area Files had to report that the origin of male dominance was poorly understood. For reasons to be explained in Chapter 1, the search slowed during the 1980s, and by the 1990s cultural studies concerning the origin of women's secondary status had nearly disappeared. According to psychologist David Buss (1996:307), feminists in many fields now tend to take patriarchy as a given without considering its origins.

Nonetheless, the study of the origin of male dominance continued to flourish in bioscience. Two disparate streams can be identified, both rooted in an evolutionary perspective. One, associated with psychology, emphasizes the physiological sex differences that correlate with gendered behaviors while attending less to the comparative historical, institutional, and economic factors that interest social scientists. Evolutionary psychologists typically see the behaviors associated with male dominance as being hormonally induced (Mealey 2000:375).

A second stream, associated with biological anthropology, emphasized the effects of ecology (e.g., the availability of food) on primate behavior. The men and women who conducted this research generally took a highly nuanced perspective on the evolutionary basis of conflicts of interest between the sexes. This body of work, cited throughout the book, is consonant with feminist goals. Below, I briefly outline an exemplary analysis that merits discussion because of its convergence with a sociological theory to be discussed a little later.

Biological anthropologist Barbara Smuts (1995:2) reports that an evolutionary analysis is entirely consistent with feminist politics. Patriarchy stems from the reproductive strategies of male primates that have been greatly elaborated in humans owing to cultural inventions like agriculture and animal husbandry and the creation of ideologies of power made possible by language. During evolution, genes are selected in an environment that includes everything that influences development inside and outside the organism, hence traits are exquisitely sensitive to environmental variation, not fixed (Smuts 1995:2, 3). While a few feminist theorists such as historian Gerda Lerner (1986) and legal philosopher Catharine MacKinnon (1987) have argued that control of female sexuality lies at the heart of patriarchy, most feminist literature focuses on how men exercise power over women. By contrast, evolutionary theory considers not only how men exercise power over women but also asks why men want such power, a question most feminists take as a given. Among mammals, conflicts of interest between the sexes stem from male interest in mate quantity and female interest in mate quality. Males may use coercion to resolve them, but very often the male does not get his way. In many primate societies male control over female sexuality is limited and in some, females are free of male sexual control (Smuts 1995:5, 8).

By contrast, human males tend to control resources and political power, which gives them more control over female sexuality than that typically found among other primates. Six conditions explain why (Smuts 1995:10–20). First, female dispersal from kin weakened female coalitions and reduced women's ability to resist male aggression. Second, male-male alliances, often directed against females, were increasingly well developed during human evolution and are of central political importance among modern humans. Third, the use of farming and animal husbandry rather than gathering and hunting to obtain food enabled males to control the resources females need to survive and reproduce, which increased male ability to coerce females. Fourth, variation in male wealth and power that perpetuated family differentials over time made women more vulnerable to the will of the most powerful men and greatly reduced their control over their sexuality. Fifth, women's need for male resources for reproduction led them to prefer resource-rich men, which contributed to male control of resources. And last, the evolution of language allowed males to propagate ideologies of male dominance–female subordination and male supremacy–female inferiority.

This analysis does not imply that our species is doomed to a patriarchal future (Smuts 1995:20). Many kinds of evidence show that human males are not genetically programmed to control women nor are women programmed to accept subordinate status. An evolutionary perspective is in agreement with perspectives that consider male coercion of females conditional rather than inevitable. Evolutionary analysis suggests that when we consider any aspect of gender inequality, we must ask how it affects female sexuality and reproduction in ways that benefit some men at the expense of women and other men.

By comparison, the sociological studies that have gone furthest in explaining the universality of women's secondary status are those that have taken a historical perspective on ecology and technology and thus could explain why the status of both sexes varies under different subsistence regimes (Lenski 1970; Blumberg 1978, 1984; Chafetz 1984, 1990). The best example of this approach is the one formulated by Randall Collins, Janet Chafetz, Rae Blumberg, Scott Coltrane, and Jonathan Turner (1993; names ordered by lot). Influenced by ecological-evolutionary theory (Lenski 1966, 1970), the theory combines biological, ecological, psychological, and sociological data. On the assumption that statistical sex differences in size, strength, and hormone levels coupled with categorical differences in reproduction are basic to women's secondary status, the authors focus on the period when human communities began to develop agriculture and animal husbandry about 10,000 years ago. Their basic observation is akin to that of Smuts: Women's secondary status is based on men's control of resources and political power rather than on fixed traits stemming from physiological sex differences. The one common reference in the two accounts is to anthropologist Ernestine Friedl's (1975) study of women and men in foraging and hoe cultures, an analysis that first fired my own interest in this topic.

Collins et al. (1993) argue that gender inequality stems from male control of resources based on the gendering of production and reproduction that is a result of sexual politics, the tendency of all-male groups to become solidaristic around masculine erotic identity. Greater size and strength and the nonfit of warfare with reproduction permit men to monopolize violence. Historically, the modern bureaucratic state eroded the political power of the extended family and the rise of individualism reduced the level of control on female behavior, but even in fully modern societies, male specialization in organized violence continues to provide a basis for sexual stereotyping and aggression. The authors conclude that it is too early to predict the outcome of the male monopoly on violence.

Thus, like Smuts (1995), the five authors (1993) argue that male solidarity in the control of female sexuality leads to the gendering of production and reproduction and the political control entailed by the male monopoly on violence. While this theory is the best extant sociological explanation of the origin and persistence of gender inequality, I do not think it is premature to predict an end to male political domination. Neither Smuts (1995) nor Collins et al. (1993) acknowledged that a nearly continuous cycle of pregnancy and lactation would facilitate the barring of women from the mainstream until the beginning of the twentieth century. The constraints of lactation were not well understood until quite late in the twentieth century. Yet, today it is difficult to avoid the conclusion that it was the ending of old-style lactation that finally enabled the mass of ordinary women to enter the political, social, and economic mainstream for the first time in human history.

In the final chapter I suggest that the male monopoly on violence may come to an end owing not only to change in the social consequences of reproductive physiology but also to alteration in the mode of governance. Modern governance is legitimated by universal suffrage. The shift from the divine right of kings to the rights of ordinary citizens tends to admit women to the political game and exclude generals, for in a modern economy characterized by a high degree of literacy, successful military command no longer provides the automatic path to political leadership that it once did and still does in the less developed nations where literacy tends to be confined to elites that exclude women. The literacy that followed upon the invention of the printing press eroded the long linkage of military and political institutions. The process required several centuries in the most developed nations and will probably not happen overnight in the others.

Why women have played little part in governance is a topic that has attracted little scholarly attention, and the answer remains unclear. Social theorists generally assume that sex differences in physiology play a part, and that these differences are immutable, for no evolutionary change has marked human bodies and brains for the past 100,000 years (Gould 1996:220). Nonetheless, while applied science has not altered human sex differences in physiology, it has irrevocably altered their social effects.

The Effect of Subsistence Technology on Human Affairs

The relationship of the reproductive process and gender equality cannot be understood without considering the historical relationship of subsistence technology to human beliefs and behaviors. Scholars generally agree that the level of equality between men and women (as well as the general level of social and political equality) was highest in the foraging groups that characterized our species for 99 percent of human history. Male dominance increased in societies based on the hoe or on herding to obtain food, and came to a peak in the great

Eurasian kingdoms and empires in the millennia when the plow was the primary tool of food production. The surplus produced by the plow tempted ambitious rulers to seize as much of it as possible, which required weapons and trained armies and resulted in a pyramidal social structure topped by a tiny elite, with peasants, serfs, and slaves massed across a wide base (Lenski 1970). Contrary to the received wisdom on the backwardness of the foraging mode, recent data demonstrate that it was the rise of agriculture, government, and urbanization that made life nasty, brutish, and short, especially for ordinary people. Levels of health plummeted, and this was nearly as true for kings and queens as for the general populace (Steckel and Rose 2002:563).

The domination of kings and emperors began to decline after a series of inventions such as the printing press and the rise of science changed the ground rules for the attainment of political and economic power. Mastery of reading enabled a better informed public to raise enough commotion to induce kings and their minions to head in another direction, and indeed an occasional head was removed as hereditary monarchies gave way to universal suffrage. The military route to political leadership remains an option today primarily in polities whose literacy rates are low. Military elites in Europe and North America have lost the political charisma they once possessed.

Not long ago, Jackson (1998) demonstrated that the migration of political and economic power from elite households to business and political interests unwittingly had increased the demand for women's services. The rapid rise in the demand for female workers was clearly a critical factor in producing the remarkable domestic and career changes that marked the lives of women in modern economies over the course of the past century.

Yet, the explanation of the increase in demand is incomplete without a corresponding analysis of the increase in supply. Only the removal of the ancient constraints of a nearly continuous cycle of pregnancy and lactation on the range of women's activities could have enabled women in large number to work outside the home. The facts about what I call old-style lactation are nearly unknown, even among the relatively few scholars who are aware of the advantages of human milk as a food for infants and young children.

The ancient practice of feeding an infant just about every 15 minutes on average began to end with the discovery of the germ theory of disease in the 1880s, the public provision of safe drinking water, and improvements in public sanitation. The ending of this mode permitted women to enter the labor market on an unprecedented scale. The shift from the ancient mode to the much less restrictive modern mode or to the bottle-feeding of cows' milk began at the instigation of women across all social classes owing to changing views of the value of time, efficiency, health, medicine, sex, and marriage, that is, the social changes concomitant with urbanization (Wolf 2001:3). Women came to doubt the efficacy, propriety, and necessity of breastfeeding. As safe drinking water became more available and mothers learned how to avoid spoiled food, bottle feeding became more common. Because of new knowledge about preparing food that was safe for infants and children, breastfeeding came to involve fewer suckling episodes over a much shorter period of time. Even the strongest proponents of maternal breastfeeding today seem unaware that their recommendations prescribe a mode that fundamentally differs from the ancient mode of lactation.

The lack of awareness of the demands that the ancient mode made on women's use of time is understandable. Only in the last years of the twentieth century did biologists come to understand the reasons for the evolutionary selection of the frequent intervals and prolonged period of suckling that had marked old-style lactation. The news has yet to spread in the social sciences, the disciplines best prepared to analyze the profound change in the mode of infant feeding that has occurred over the past century. The physiology of pregnancy and lactation are unchanged, but applied science now enables women to avoid the cycle of nearly continuous pregnancy and lactation that sexual intercourse imposed on earlier generations.

Data concerning pregnancy and lactation are scattered across many disciplines. Integrating such data with social science research provides huge opportunity for error. Plans for new research tend to recommend interdisciplinary research, often casually, as though the benefits were obvious, but such advice ignores the costs of dabbling in someone else's business. Interdisciplinary work all too easily becomes undisciplined work (Haaga 2003:507), and the deep divide between biology and social science forestalls the emergence of a network that might link disparate areas (Collins 1998).

But the game matters. The sexual division of labor began with male inability to feed an infant the only food it could digest. Modern technology did not alter sex differences in human physiology; it changed the social effects of those differences. Men can fly without wings and can feed infants though their breasts yield no milk. The lopsided differential in the ability to rear human infants has evanesced. As Jonathan Turner (1985:11) observed in another context, population maintenance as a force of macrolevel social organization needs to be brought back into the core of sociological theory. This book explains how it came to be that frequent and prolonged lactation played a central role in the persistence of gender stratification. It was human culture that once enabled men to become more dominant politically than the males of any other primate species (Smuts 1995). Ironically, it is human culture that has now created the conditions for women to play an equal part.

Chapter One

Why the Search for Human Origins Stumbled

FROM A SOCIOLOGIST'S PERSPECTIVE, anthropologists' search for the origins of gender inequality appeared to peak in the early 1970s and then slow nearly to a halt. But it was only the search conducted in cultural anthropology, the area of the discipline with which sociologists are most familiar, that peaked and declined. Spurred by the renewal of feminism in the late 1960s and the rise in the number of women in social sciences and humanities a little later, many cultural anthropologists had wanted to know why women's subordination to men seemed to be universal.

Despite cultural anthropologists' involvement in human origins research in the 1970s, many of them were leery of biological explanations. It had been a biological perspective that led European anthropologists to explain group differences in racist terms. Early in the twentieth century Franz Boas urged colleagues to use the concept of culture instead of race to explain group differences lest American anthropology take the route of its French and German counterparts. Other social scientists resisted imports from biology owing to the legacy of eugenics and Social Darwinism, better named Social Spencerism, for unmerciful competition was praised as depicting what Darwin actually had taught (Mayr 1982:883; Haaga 2002:515). The exclusion of biology ultimately led to the Standard Social Science Model, the idea that human culture was solely a product of history and environment, not reducible to biology or psychology (Wilson 1998:188).

Thus, the time span of the search for origins conducted in anthropology as a whole was brief. The most likely reason it petered out is that the divide between biological and cultural anthropology, the fields that comprised the intellectual center of the search, had become a deep chasm by the mid-1980s. Two new trends that shared no elective affinities, sociobiology and postmodernism, pushed biological and cultural anthropology in opposite directions. Scholarly exchange became difficult, which deprived other disciplines of anthropological syntheses that might have explained the consequences of the interaction of biology and culture, especially after humans invented farming 10,000 years ago.

The new theory of sociobiology stirred the imaginations of biological anthropologists. The focus on the evolution of animal behavior was a giant step forward in all of biology, for it demonstrated a way to measure the evolutionary aspects of an animal's reproductive behavior. The reception of sociobiology in the social sciences was muted owing to a careless application of the findings about animals to humans and a flavor of Victorian sexism that disturbed feminists, including those who did biological research. The claim that anthropology and sociology could be subsumed under sociobiology probably displeased most social scientists. By the late 1970s, sociobiology was a favorite target of academic radicals. By the mid-1980s, only a plurality in the cultural field accepted sociobiology's central concepts even though it had become biological anthropology's most basic perspective (Lieberman 1989).

By contrast, the postmodernist trend primarily affected disciplines in the humanities as well as areas of social science that emphasized description and interpretation. Postmodernism held that there was no truth. There was only text. The material world was irrelevant. Intensifying the perception of many social scientists that racism and sexism were inherent in biological research, the postmodernist rejection of science helped to bring about the dissolution of the search for human origins in cultural anthropology.

Yet, despite the chasm created by the polar perspectives of sociobiology and postmodernism, the four fields of anthropology at that time were much alike in one respect. Archeology, biological anthropology, cultural anthropology, and linguistics together comprised a no-woman's land. The research faculty, mostly male, had given scant attention to what women thought, what they contributed to subsistence, and how they nourished their children. A two-sex perspective on human origins would require a significant substantive contribution.

In recounting the search for human origins, I introduce sociobiology first, a little out of order, for it appeared in 1975. However, it is basic to the understanding of modern biology. I then discuss the male model of human origins, the search for a two-sex model, the effect of postmodernism on interpretive studies, the virtual ending of the search for origins, and the costs of excluding biology in explanations of human thought and behavior.

Sociobiology

Sociobiology, introduced by Harvard entomologist Edward Wilson (1975), applied natural selection theory to the behavioral aspects of reproduction. The explanation of animal reproductive behavior assumes that the purpose of the behavior is to maximize individual reproductive success (Konner 1982:15). The theory of sociobiology held that the evolutionary success of individuals is measured by the quality of fitness, defined as the number of an individual's offspring who live long enough to reproduce. The individual who is most fit is the one who contributes the most genes to the next generation. Sociobiology thus differed profoundly from theories holding that natural selection benefited the species rather than the individual. The emphasis on the individual provided a way to engage in far more precise measurement, and the new theory spawned a flood of research that elegantly explained evolutionary aspects of nonhuman animal behavior. The theory is widely accepted today in all of the biological sciences.

In the light of subsequent criticism, it was ironic that Wilson (1975:551) began by claiming that the handling of genetics by Konrad Lorenz, Lionel Tiger, Robin Fox, Robert Ardrey, and Desmond Morris, who emphasized the inevitability of male dominance, was inefficient and misleading. Based on a review of a small sample of animal species, these authors would select a plausible hypothesis, then *advocate* it to the limit [Wilson's italics], though real theory must be deductive and testable. In *The Imperial Animal*, for example, Tiger and Fox (1971) did not formulate their theory about human male behavior in a falsifiable form. The substitution of advocacy for strong inference makes science nothing but a wide open game that any number can play (Wilson 1975:29).

Despite Wilson's advocacy of the scientific method, sociobiology intensified social science skepticism about biology and deepened the divide between anthropology's cultural and biological fields. Over time, the label became so politicized that many biological scientists would refer to research on animals as behavioral ecology and that on humans as evolutionary psychology (Zuk 2002:1). Four aspects of sociobiology especially troubled social scientists.

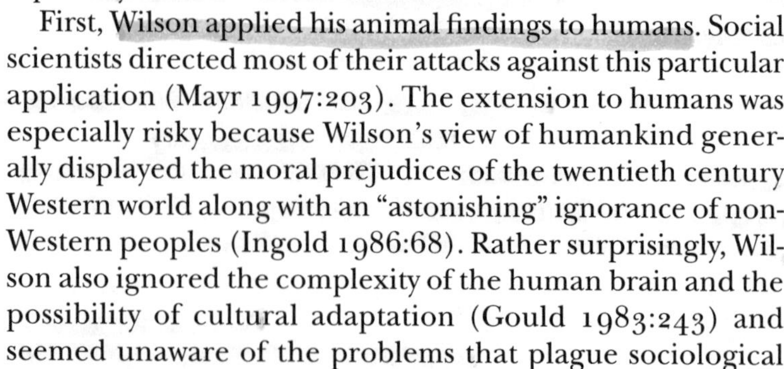

First, Wilson applied his animal findings to humans. Social scientists directed most of their attacks against this particular application (Mayr 1997:203). The extension to humans was especially risky because Wilson's view of humankind generally displayed the moral prejudices of the twentieth century Western world along with an "astonishing" ignorance of non-Western peoples (Ingold 1986:68). Rather surprisingly, Wilson also ignored the complexity of the human brain and the possibility of cultural adaptation (Gould 1983:243) and seemed unaware of the problems that plague sociological explanation. Discussing insects with many facts, Wilson would say nothing about humans. Speaking about humans with few facts, he used insect behavior to make critical points (Washburn 1978:60). The theory explained the behavior of nonhuman primates and other animals. The application to humans clearly needed more work. Relating zoological definitions of power to definitions of power developed for humans is problematic: Human notions of social power rarely consider the currency of reproduction (Smuts 1995:24).

Second, applying the model to humans highlighted a problem obvious to demographers. The theory ignored the worldwide decline in human fertility. Though the abrupt change in the association between wealth and fertility requires explanation (see Kaplan and Lancaster 2000:317; 2003), there is no evolutionary rationale for the demographic transition (Luttberg, Borgerhoff, Mangel 2000:364). A major challenge facing sociobiology, evolutionary psychology, and human behavioral ecology is the extent to which these areas can explain the changes in human sexual behavior over the past 200 years, especially the decline to extremely low levels of fertility (Hobcraft 2003:340). As Cavalli-Sforza (2000:205) recently noted, cultural development has slowed biological evolution. The effect of natural selection on fertility and mortality has been the greatest evolutionary factor in human biology, but modern medicine has so reduced prereproductive mortality that demographic growth must be sharply curtailed to prevent serious overpopulation.

A large body of data demonstrates that the demographic transition turned the effect of wealth on fertility upside down, for the rich generally got richer and the poor got children. One problem in producing an explanation is that the shorthand used to describe copulation does not accurately state why an animal engages in sexual activity. The language of sociobiology implies that individuals copulate for the sake of fitness. Sociobiologists agree, however, that no animal knows in any cognitive sense why it behaves as it does. Natural selection in the course of evolution simply results in an animal's behaving as if it wanted offspring (Konner 1982:268). An impartial observer of copulation in nonhuman mammals might conclude that the purpose of the behavior is to attain sexual satisfaction. Offspring are a byproduct. In humans, the byproduct may be welcome or unwelcome.

A related problem is that sociobiologists often discuss Darwinian selection as if only individual characteristics determine reproductive success. This view ignores the environment, which Darwin made the critical determinant of selection (Potts 1996:227). Animals copulate in pursuit of sexual satisfaction in a particular environment. For most animals, it tends to be a given, but not for humans, who can rapidly change their environment in a brief period of time, as happened during the industrial revolution. Urban living, education, and a cornucopial proliferation of material goods gave most humans an incentive to restrict the number of children they wanted to rear. Because young adults evolved from a mammal species are equipped with a strong sexual urge, they often experience a desire to copulate. They may on occasion hope to demonstrate their fitness but, apparently, more often, not. Henry Ford's career exemplifies an unintended effect of environmental change on human behavior. Ford invented the assembly line and paid workers good wages to enable them to buy cars, which gave adolescents a home away from home. Booming car sales induced chemists to improve rubber tires, and improved rubber technology led to a better condom. (Like college diplomas, the Roman originals had been made of sheepskin.) An unexpected consequence of assembly line production gave American adolescents the privacy and means to separate procreation and recreation.

Third, the sociobiological account of the differing sexual strategies of human males and females, often stated in language with sexist overtones, highlighted the difficulties inherent in using the sexual strategies of other mammals to explain human behavior. Like their nonhuman counterparts, human males have zillions of sperm while females have far fewer eggs. Male strategy calls for a man to deposit his sperm in as many females as he can. By contrast, a woman should be choosy, picking a man who might stick around and help feed the kiddies. The sociobiological literature usually describes her mien while waiting around for Mr. Right as "coy." However, were males choosy about mates, would they be called coy or judicious (Cronin 1991:248)?

Applied to humans, sociobiology seemed akin to a post-sexual revolution version of Victorian sexism (Small 1993:91). Thus, when sociologist Pierre van den Berghe (1978:197) introduced sociobiology to colleagues, he assured them that the theory supported the conventional wisdom on family sex roles: It is natural for papa to wear the pants. Moreover, the castrating female is no myth: A woman can threaten a man to the point of sexual dysfunction should she assume the dominant role.

Sociobiologists have generally characterized female sexuality as less intense and less oriented toward variety than male sexuality. Yet, were female sexuality so limited, men would not need to try so hard to control it. Women can gain benefits from mating with multiple partners. Evidence from primates and relatively unconstrained women reveals an assertive female sexuality excited by variety (Smuts 1996:255).

Fourth, perhaps to help subsume the social sciences under sociobiology, Wilson introduced a concept intended to give these disciplines a firm scientific foundation. In *Genes, Mind, and Culture,* Lumsden and Wilson (1981:99, 368) proposed a concept they called the culturgen to explain cultural evolution, parallel to the part played by the gene in biological evolution. Akin to the meme and an analog of the gene, the culturgen is an idea, tune, or catch phrase that propagates itself by leaping from brain to brain, the means of cultural transmission in a process parallel to biological evolution according to Dawkins

(1976:192). The gene made biology a science by showing how natural selection actually worked. The culturgen could do the same for social science.

But it was not to be. The so-called evolution of culture, unlike biological evolution, is not based on random selection of units (Cavalli-Sforza and Feldman 1981:357, 70; see also Ingold 1986). The mode of transmission clearly differentiates genetic from cultural evolution. Memes and culturgens would have meaning only if categories were discontinuous, as are atoms, genes, and DNA. Cultural transmission has never been analyzed in any depth (Cavalli-Sforza and Cavalli-Sforza 1995:224). Despite a recent attempt to show how culture and biological evolution are related (Richerson and Boyd 2005), the key problem remains.

A theory of cultural transmission based on individualistic psychology omits too many causal factors to be a functional analog of the gene in genetic evolution. Functionalist theories of sociology and anthropology that often explicitly claimed to be Darwinian have been notoriously vague about the mechanisms by which the higher-level good prevailed over individual selfishness (Cronin 1991:370). Cultural "mutations" may result from random events and thus be similar to genetic mutations, but cultural changes are more often intentional or directed to a specific goal, while biological mutations are blind to their potential benefit (Cavalli-Sforza 2000:176). Among our kind, armed conflict, social stratification, and ideology deeply affect cultural outcomes. In a given conflict, who will be the masters, who, the slaves? And why? Untangling causality in human affairs is more complicated than some sociobiologists seem to think.

In the opinion of the twentieth century's greatest biologist, the misconception that Spencer's evolutionism is like Darwin's has been a great handicap to both anthropology and sociology (Mayr 1982:494). Cultural evolution implies parallels with natural evolution that do not exist. "Cultural change" (Gould 1996:219) or "Spencerian selection" (Turner 1995:16) might be more accurate.

The Male Model

In retrospect, it is fair to observe that the male models of human evolution in the 1960s played a large role in motivating feminists and sympathizers to produce a body of work that showed in detail why one-sex models of human origins were inadequate. The theories of human nature promulgated in the 1960s and 1970s attempted to demonstrate that biology made male dominance inevitable. A consequence was that the rising numbers of women students in anthropology graduate departments had to suffer through "mortifying" years of hearing about man the hunter and the political superiorities of men in groups (Hrdy 1990:35). The models of early man produced by anthropologists and primatologists were embedded in a masculinist ideology, and they appeared just when women's struggle for inclusion in academia was sensitizing graduate students to the personal and political costs of claims that cast doubt on women's capacity to operate as well as men did outside the home. As Zuk (2002:201) said later, it is not the science of biology that harms women; it is the human misuse of that science.

Probably the best known male model of human origins was that of man the hunter, which dominated scholarly and popular writing in the 1960s. Some authors claimed that primate males were biologically designed to dominate the group life of their species. All human life, intellect, and emotions were said to have evolved from the adaptation to hunting that also hardwired predatory aggression into male nature (Washburn and Lancaster 1968:292).

In the 1970s, scholars of both sexes challenged the model. As it turned out, man the hunter (see Chapter 2) had a short shelf life. By the 1980s primatologists (many of them women by then) were laying him gently to rest (see Fedigan 1986). No conclusive proof demonstrated that dominance was highly heritable or that dominant male primates sired the most infants (Fedigan 1992:280). The rank order of most mammals can be determined simply by weighing individuals, save for monkeys and apes, whose rank ordering often does not correlate with their physical power (Byrne 1995:199).

The scholars who heard the news of the hunter's demise included few students of gender, for most of them had already given up on biology. Lopreato and Crippen (1999) have reported that the current feminist literature agrees that biology cannot explain cultural sex differences even in part. The claim was overstated, for it excluded work like that of Rossi (1983) and Collins, Chafetz, Blumberg, Coltrane, and Turner (1993), but not by much.

The Search for a Two-Sex Model

From a sociological perspective, an obvious place to begin a search for data on the behaviors and beliefs that characterize preliterate societies was in cultural and archeological anthropology, especially in studies that focused on the ecology and technology of food production. Sociologist Gerhard Lenski's (1966, 1970) theory of social stratification, based on an ecological-subsistence perspective, covered a wide range of societies. It was the first to make data in anthropology accessible to other social scientists (Mosley and Wallerstein 1978). The theory drew extensively on the research of cultural anthropologists, but they did not often cite it. The largest body of research in cultural anthropology depended on the concept of culture to explain societal variation though a number of anthropologists had long focused on the effects of environment and subsistence, especially among foragers (Heider 1972; Kelly 1995:6).

Early on, Franz Boas had introduced the concept of culture to combat intellectual and political racism. Racism rose to an historical high worldwide in the nineteenth century owing to the confluence of three disparate factors: the idea of the survival of the fittest (a bastardized version of Darwinist thought), the superiority of Northwest European military hardware, and the physical characteristics (evolved to permit climatic adaptation) that made different groups identifiable (van den Berghe 1967). Observers could readily identify a variety of "natives" from European invaders. The conquerors invented a ready explanation to justify their behavior: The natives were subhuman.

After emerging among military and business elites in response to the Northern European conquest of lands across the globe, the idea that natives were inferior by nature seeped into anthropology, which got a disciplinary boost when European elites needed to know what made the natives restless. Theories that confounded race with the so-called stages of evolution soon dominated the new discipline. Anthropologists decided that primitive peoples were simply less evolved (Stocking 1968:307).

To avoid ancestral error, many twentieth-century American anthropologists followed Boas in using the concept of culture to explain societal variation lest racism triumph as it had in German and French anthropology (Harris 1969:297; Degler 1991:84). The exclusion of biology brought about an extreme in environmentalism that had its magnificent heyday when the excesses of genetic determinism threatened not only human dignity but also human survival in areas of Nazi domination during World War II. Cultural determinism thus had served a good purpose and was for many years a respectable position (Konner 1982:105).

Nonetheless, the use of the concept of culture to explain societal variation incurred costs. Probably the most important one resulted from promoting the belief that each society is unique, which implies that general theory can explain no traits nor can most studies serve as sources in cross-cultural research (Udy 1973:253). Unsurprisingly, the study of human universals was taboo most of the twentieth century (Brown 1991:6). Cultural anthropologists tended to focus on particulars in field data, leave theoretical issues implicit, and give short shrift to the methods required by comparative studies (Goody 1962:v).

Despite such problems, the entry of increasing numbers of women into anthropology departments in the 1970s led women anthropologists to question how it came to be that women occupied a second class status everywhere, save for the possible exception of foraging groups. Because anthropology embraces scientific, social-scientific, and humanities modes of interpretation, feminists have worked in every part of the globe and in every specialized subfield, from primates to politics. Women in anthropology thus acquired a strong sense that the results of their work were of key importance to feminist political decisionmaking (di Leonardo 1991:1, 3).

By the mid-1970s a number of women representing a variety of theoretical views had produced an entire new literature on the status of women across cultures and had played a key intellectual role in the redefining of women's place in the evolution of human society (Quinn 1977:181). Both cultural and physical anthropologists provided data that showed in detail how the lack of information on female activities had led to erroneous conclusions about the inevitability of male dominance (see references in Haraway 1989:298). Yet, a comprehensive review of studies concerning the origins of women's status published in the prestigious *Annual Review of Anthropology* reported that the findings were inconclusive (Quinn 1977:183). However, Quinn noted that the literature had produced three generalizations: men's universal monopoly over formal political office, women's exclusion from prestige spheres, and universal ideologies of sex differences favoring men. These three propositions provided a fertile and suggestive point of departure for future research that was rarely used.

A new review a decade later reflected a great deepening of the chasm separating biological and cultural anthropology, though the cleavage was made less apparent by the tendency of scholars in both fields to call themselves "anthropologists." A review in the *Annual Review of Anthropology* again reported that gender asymmetry was still unexplained despite the huge outpouring of literature on women's cross-cultural position over a ten-year period (Mukhopadhyay and Higgins 1988). Whyte's (1978) study, based on the problematic Murdock sample (Fedigan 1986:247) had dampened enthusiasm for macromodels. Despite the domination of gender issues in the literature during the 1980s, the reasons for women's absence from political and military arenas were still little studied (Ross 1986:844). No one pursued Friedl's (1975) suggestion that the male monopoly on warfare was a consequence of men's greater expendability, nor had anyone addressed men's monopoly on political affairs or women's exclusion from institutionalized competition for prestige noted in the earlier review. According to the authors, there was only a profound realization that the original questions still lacked answers and might even have been naive and inappropriate.

A little later, di Leonardo (1991:vii) declared that the universality of sexual asymmetry was no longer a central question in anthropology. Cultural anthropologists seemingly gave up on the search for the origins of gender inequality. Antiestablishment theorists celebrated women's differences and even refused to see women as a unitary social category (Scheppele 1994:393). Studies of the origins of human behavior were seen as fraught with sexism and racism.

The doctrine of Platonic essentialism was resurrected and given a new twist that turned its meaning upside down. For example, Rosaldo (1980:392) claimed that the search for human origins is based on the assumption that the roots of gender systems are essentially unchanging, and declared the search itself revealed a faith in ultimate and essential truths. Yet, the extent to which the roots of social systems do or do not change is a matter for research, not faith. Rosaldo's view reflects confusion about science, for scientists agree that there are no ultimate and essential truths, and Rosaldo wrongly implied that essentialism is acceptable in science. The doctrine of Platonic essentialism, which long dominated Western thought, held that appearances are based on underlying essences that comprise the only permanent reality. This view makes science impossible. Platonic essentialism was ended by the rise of biology in the 1800s (Mayr 1982:38). The power of Platonic essentialism is due in part to the fact that it fit the tenets of creationism so well. The two dogmas reinforced one another (Mayr 1978:18).

Enter Postmodernism

By the 1990s, a postmodernist trend swept across departments of English and history and into the areas of social science that emphasized interpretation. Science was nothing but ideology. Causal analysis was out. The new fancy of the academic left, postmodernism had an elective affinity with the idea that reality was a social construction (Segerstrale 2000:308). The so-called social construction of reality, which held that reality is only what we think about it, was based on a faulty interpretation of a popular book of that name, for Berger and Luckman (1966) had carefully explained that they did not reject the idea of a real world independent of human observation. Psychologist John Money (1995:30) claimed that social constructionism was a cosmetic name change for sociocultural theory, a name for a new brand of politically correct scholarship for intellectual kindred in newly established divisions of feminist, ethnic, gay and lesbian, and minority studies in the humanities. The sole emphasis on recreational sex in constructionist models of sexuality neatly avoided reproductive biology, but the new models were as time and culture bound as the earlier theories they criticized (Rossi 1994:6).

Postmodernism defies common definition even by those who claim to practice it (Scheppele 1994:397). Flax (1987:623) asserted that it includes feminist theory, which may be true. Coherent statements of feminist theory and epistemology are rare (Rule 1997:157). Moreover, the ideas in so-called feminist epistemology were not raised by women and many feminist sociologists do not agree with them (Chafetz 1997:99). *Soi-disant* feminist ethnography is an amalgam of identity politics and postmodernism (di Leonardo 1998:310).

What matters in postmodernism is the text. There is no truth. There is only the endless unraveling of text. As textual analysis trumps empirical data, postmodernism implies that a rational sociology of science is impossible. Radical feminists would throw out the edifice of science and start again. Postmodern feminists would deny that such an edifice was possible. Why, asks John Maynard Smith (1997:522–6), do they expect the light to go on when they press the switch? Yet, the antiscience trend in anthropology had some devastating effects. The denigration of science, for example, created an atmosphere that made it impossible to measure morbidity and mortality outcomes of racist public policies among indigenous South American peoples (Hill and Hurtado 1996:478).

Not all cultural anthropologists accepted these ideas, of course, but the number who did sufficed to reorient the field. Causal thinking about the material world became less common. Ethnography came to be seen more as literary endeavor than science. These trends nearly wiped out replicable research in cultural anthropology. By the 1990s, most research on the origins of human behavior was conducted only in disciplines oriented to biological science.

The Cost of Excluding Biodata

The exclusion of biological data from theories addressed to gender inequality has harmed scholarship, first, by forestalling study of an activity that curtailed the range of women's activities in the premodern period. As late as 1979 the average time worldwide of cessation of breastfeeding was 4.2 years (Lawrence and Lawrence 1999:336). Second, ignoring biodata foreclosed the study of the only sex differences that are irreducible and nonoverlapping, those of procreation (Money 1995:53). Only men impregnate. Only women menstruate, ovulate, gestate, and lactate. Other biological sex differences (testosterone levels, body size and strength, brains, cognition, sex hormones) lie on an overlapping continuum such that some women possess more of a male sex attribute like body strength and size than do most men. All societies divide those who can bear and nourish children from those who cannot, though a few add a category for those unable to bear children but unfitted for whatever is defined as the male role (Schlegel 1990:39). Complete sex change in mammals is impossible. Some humans have changed sex socially, legally, hormonally, and surgically, but they cannot breed in the sex they adopt (Money 1995:52). Unlike other primates, the sexual dimorphism that matters in humans is not the anatomy of aggression (bone, muscle, canine teeth) but rather the storage of fat to support nearly continuous lactation in the adult female (Lancaster 1985:22).

The most basic problem with the rejection of biology is that the dichotomy of biology and culture is as misguided as that between body and mind. Mental and physical cannot be neatly separated. The mental is simply a set of physical features of the brain at a higher level of description than that of neurons (Searle 1995:227). To assess what proportion of a given mental or behavioral outcome results from biology and what percent from culture is futile. A complex system of feedbacks connects biology and culture (Konner 1982:89). Poison in the human diet causes phenylketonuria. If the poison is removed, the disorder will not appear even if the abnormal genes that activated it remain. Phenylketonuria is thus a disease of the mind that is totally genetic and totally environmental at the same time. No better evidence can show the folly of partitioning mental and behavioral characteristics into percentages of genetic and environmental causation.

Chapter Two

From Primates to Humans

IN THIS REVIEW I discuss the contributions of a relatively new discipline, primatology, to research concerning the origins of human behavior. Most feminist analyses of the origins of male domination begin no earlier than the emergence of farming about 10,000 years ago, but the origins, which are far more ancient, stem from sex differences in mammal behavior owing to differences in the ways males and females reproduce. Biologists agree that males are more interested in mate quantity while females care more about mate quality. The conflict of interest can be reduced if a male offers a female desired benefits, but the benefits that make a difference tend to be costly in male time and energy.

According to biological anthropologist Barbara Smuts (1995:2), patriarchy (the extension of male sex dominance over society) is the product of typical male primate reproductive strategies that have been elaborated in our species. For social scientists, this view implies the need to consider the interaction of adaptive traits with particular institutional environments, with particular emphasis on subsistence technology.

However, with a few exceptions such as Tanner and Zihlman (1976) and Zihlman (1978), research on the evolution of humans and their nearest cousins played relatively little part in the standard academic repertoire in women's studies, the humanities, and the social sciences owing to an exclusion of biodata that began early in the 1900s. Anthropologists used the concept of culture instead of race to explain societal variation, and other social scientists fell into step. The idea that human arrangements were social constructions helped to define an appropriate area for relatively new disciplines like sociology, while the avoidance of racism yielded a pleasing sense of moral superiority (Huber 2004).

Though the evolutionary studies of the 1960s and 1970s were not racist, their affinity with sexism was evident. Masculinist ideology permeated studies of human origins. Well into the 1980s most behavioral biologists described males as aggressive and promiscuous; females, as passive and coy. The bias was especially obvious in reconstructions of human evolution and popular versions of the human implications of research on the behavior of other animals (Hrdy and Williams 1983:3).

Field workers in primatology had focused on males, save for mother-infant relations. In most primate groups, males were said to determine the social structure by means of a hierarchy that depended on their power to maintain order. These ideas persisted in anthropology textbooks and in popular writing long after the central role of female primates in determining social structure had been well documented (Hrdy and Williams, 1983:5).[1] By the late 1980s, however, a female perspective had become part of the structure of primatology such that the field is sometimes singled out for praise as an "equal opportunity" science (Fedigan 1992:xii).

Yet few feminists outside of the biological sciences were aware that male-centered ideology was disappearing from biological research during the 1980s because many feminists had come to avoid not only biology but all of science as well owing to the effects of an intellectual fad imported from France. Postmodernist theory held that there was no truth, only an endless unraveling of text, and the mounds of ravels soon grew into mountains of obfuscation. Below, I discuss the problem of ideology that marked the work of early primatologists in order to explain why it disturbed feminists. I end with a discussion of evolutionary issues that are currently unresolved.

Who Are the Primates?

Below, I introduce the primates and the primatologists, then discuss some highly influential studies as well as several popular presentations published in the 1960s and 1970s. In retrospect, it seems likely that these analyses written for a popular audience were so obviously ideological that they incited a reaction opposite to what their authors intended: They stimulated feminist scholars, both male and female, to ensure that good science would prevail over the long run.

Save for humans, the primates comprise a relatively unsuccessful and small group of mammals (Rowell 1972:20). The first representatives of the order appeared about 70 million years ago. As they proliferated and expanded geographically, they attained their heyday 50 to 60 million years ago. The order then became relatively insignificant until less than 12,000 years ago when one species, our own, domesticated plants and animals and peopled the earth (Lancaster 1975:5).

Primate categories often change, for they must be amended often to accommodate new research findings. According to Tuttle (2001:178), the subdivision of the category that divides monkeys, apes, and humans into families, subfamilies, tribes, genera, and other Linnaean categories will continue to be contentious. Schemes that are based on comparative morphology of extant forms and a few fossil bits face formidable challenges both from molecular biologists who expect uniform and objective classification to be based on times of species divergence (genetic distance) and from a new generation of paleo-primatologists backed by phalanxes of new and fortified fossil species.

The Primate Order includes prosimians (the so-called lower primates: lemurs, lorises, tarsiers) and anthropoids (the higher primates: monkeys, apes, and humans). According to de Waal (2001:2), new world monkeys branched off from old world monkeys about 35 million years ago (mya). A little more than 20 mya the hominoids (apes and humans) branched off from Old World monkeys. Orangutans split from the Hominoid line about 10 mya; gorillas, about 7 mya; chimpanzees, about 5 mya. After splitting off from us, chimpanzees and bonobos diverged about 2 mya. These two species are our closest relatives among living species, and we are equally close to both.

Anatomically modern humans and their fossil relatives as well as the great apes of Africa and Asia (bonobos, chimpanzees, gorillas, and orangutans), and the lesser apes (gibbons and siamangs) traditionally belonged to the same superfamily, the Hominoidea, but we modern humans and the great apes belong to separate families, the Hominidae and the Pongidae. Whether or not a primatologist assigns great apes and humans to the same family depends on personal preferences in taxonomic classification. Apes and humans are now seen as being much closer than was previously thought, but lumping them into one genus will be a bitter pill for those who like to think of humans as something special, even for scientists who espouse a cladistic perspective (Diamond 1992:75).

Our line includes fossils with fancy names as well as our own species, Homo sapiens sapiens (anatomically modern humans). Other species in the line have disappeared, and our own prospects for survival seem only so-so. As mathematician Tom Lehrer (1986) put it during the Cold War in the 1950s, "When the bomb that drops on you gets your friends and neighbors too, we will all go together when we go." It is mildly comforting to know that we haven't gone yet.

Nonhuman primates are now in serious danger of extinction owing to loss of habitat, described in a series of well-researched essays published by the Smithsonian Institution (Beck et al. 2001). Primates evolved in areas warm and wet enough to supply food such as fruits, leaves, and small animals. Most (but not all) nonhuman primates continue to live in tropical countries where they compete with expanding human populations who typically live in areas that are relatively undeveloped economically.

In Africa a large primate population was sustainable until the 1950s when the human population increased rapidly with the reduction of diseases like malaria. Western technologies capable of destroying apes and their forest habitats were widely used. Current forest destruction in Africa, Asia, and South America is high, but Africa loses forests faster (Butynski 2001:25; Mittermeier and Cheney 1987). The basic cause of the decline of Africa's apes is the poverty of the continent's rapidly expanding human population. Curbing the growth of human populations to bring them in line with a sustainable use of natural resources requires consistent governmental implementation of population policy, something that no African nation has been able to accomplish (Butynski 2001:39).

Primates have the greatest range in social organization known in any vertebrate order (Janson 1992:5). The primate order includes species that are solitary, monogamous, harem-like, multimale, promiscuous, polyandrous, and that live in extended cooperative families (so-called fission-fusion structures). Individuals join and leave temporary subgroups formed by a larger community of individuals. Primatologists agree that social variation within or between species may relate to differences in ecological or sociodemographic variables. For example, nocturnal species tend to be solitary because their food sources, insects, are dispersed and scarce (Janson 1992:97).

Yet, despite general agreement on the costs and benefits of sociality for primates, the relative importance of various ecological factors in shaping social systems across species remains unknown to a large degree. The scarcity of focused quantitative socioecological studies makes it very hard to compare the intensity of even a single factor such as the competition for food across many species (Janson 1992).

It was once widely believed that only humans made and used tools, but Jane Goodall's research upset that idea. Chimpanzee tool use exceeds in variety and complexity all that has been reported for all other animals except humans, and chimpanzees are fully capable of transmitting this behavior across generations. They (usually the females) use straw or stick probes to collect termites from nests, stones to bash open hard-shelled fruits, sticks and twigs to pick their teeth, and have even been observed using leaves to wipe themselves after defecation (Lancaster 1975:52). Chimpanzees also have culture. They can adopt behavior patterns that seem useful such as washing the sand off potatoes before eating them (McGrew 2001).

However, chimpanzee tool use is awkward, like that of a human child (Washburn 1968:38). The evolution of an apparently simple motor skill such as throwing depends on the activity's being pleasurable, rewarding, and practiced in play. For example, when angry chimpanzees throw rocks at other animals, they aim without skill and consistently miss the target. Caged with nothing to do, their throwing of feces may become quite accurate.

To better understand the steps in the transition to human culture, McGrew (2001:254) suggests that the perspectives of comparative psychology and behavioral ecology be joined to those of cultural anthropology and archaeology. Cultural primatology, a new synthesis of theory and methods, would cross the boundaries of the social and natural sciences.

And Who Are the Primatologists?

Primatologists comprise a rather small crew, for their young discipline blossomed only in the last half of the twentieth century. According to DeVore (1965:vii), almost nothing systematic was known about the natural behavior of a single monkey or ape until C. R. Carpenter at Penn State began his study of the howler monkeys of Panama in 1931. After that, save for Carpenter's pioneering work on the howler, gibbon, and rhesus and a few other studies, primate field studies lay dormant for nearly 20 years. The modern period of such studies, which emphasized long-term careful observation, began in the mid-1950s. Scholars at Kyoto University established the Japan Monkey Center, and Stuart Altmann undertook a two-year restudy of the rhesus monkey colony on Cayo Santiago off Puerto Rico.

Primatologists are a singular lot among zoologists, for primates are few compared to the huge numbers in other animal species (Rowell 1999). Worse, captive primates are costly to keep. In the wild they are mostly on lists of endangered species. Students must be willing to study them over long periods for they live long lives in small groups, and if the account is to be accurate, the study must continue for years.

Unlike zoologists, most students of primate behavior are grounded in the social sciences. In the United States, almost all of them are located in anthropology departments. According to Rowell (1999:7), this outcome is mostly due to the organizational genius of anthropologist Sherwood Washburn at the University of California, Berkeley. In the early 1960s Washburn managed to parlay a renewed interest in human origins and the human past into actual money for studies of primate behavior in both field and laboratory.

Primatologists trained as anthropologists often study nonhuman primates with an eye to casting light on the behavior of our own species (Fedigan 1986:38). The study of our nearest cousins can help to explain how we differ from them and how we are alike. Inferences drawn from animals to humans make many primatologists uncomfortable with the overly facile analogies that have been made in the past, but there is pressure from both colleagues and the public to make primate studies more directly relevant to the study of humans. There are now relatively more women in primatology than in related disciplines. Women earn four-fifths of the PhDs (Schiebinger 1999:27), and feminist critiques have strongly influenced primatology and biological anthropology (di Leonardo 1991:7).

The Problem of Ideology

When university research faculties were mostly male, the findings tended to reflect the ideas of the male-dominated wider society concerning appropriate gender behaviors. “Tend” is a key word. The extent to which scientists can overcome their own biases of place and time varies enormously. It is hard for investigators to rid themselves of preconceived notions absent strong and specific evidence to the contrary.

Darwin himself demonstrated how hard it can be to overcome the dominant ideology of a particular time and place. The difficulty was evidenced not by his seemingly logical proposal that bipedal locomotion, brain enlargement, and tool use emerged together as the hominids evolved, for upright stance freed the hands to make and use tools, which required more intelligence that led to larger brains and even better tools. The bias lay in Darwin's failure explicitly to include women among the tool users (Fedigan 1986).

In fact, Darwin said little about women's place. When he did speak of it, he left undisturbed the received wisdom of Victorian England: Man is more powerful in body and mind than woman, and in the savage state he keeps her in a far more abject state of bondage than does the male of any other animal. Biological processes had selected for courageous, intelligent, tool-using men (Darwin 1936:901). Not knowing how traits were transmitted to the next generation, Darwin created a concept he called "equal transmission of characters" to explain why women were not left totally behind. Fortunately, he opined, the law of equal transmission to both sexes prevails among all mammals. Were it not so, man probably would have become as superior to woman in mental endowment as the peacock is to the peahen in ornamental plumage (Darwin 1936:874; Fedigan 1986:29).

Later, Darwin's ideas on social evolution were largely forgotten. The idea that all societies were evolving toward the goal of European civilization had become offensive in a discipline founded on the premise of cultural relativity (Fedigan 1986:31). The discovery that hominids were bipedal long before the first detectable stone tools appeared decoupled Darwin's trinity of bipedalism, tool use, and brain expansion in any simple form (Tooby and DeVore 1987:203). After a century of speculation, paleobiologists reported that our australopithecine ancestors had become bipedal long before the brain attained its current size. Bipedalism, tool use, and brain enlargement had emerged separately over extended periods. Conclusive evidence from Laetoli and Ethiapi showed that the earliest known hominids were undeniably bipedal by 3.7 million years ago but they had very small brains, only a little larger than the brains of their ape cousins (Reader 1998:61). At that juncture in their evolutionary history, they did not use stone tools although, after the fashion of chimpanzees, they might have used sticks, stones, and bones as tools.

In the 1960s, anthropologists' interest in the evolution of human origins over the long period in which our species diverged from other apes highlighted the problem of ideology. Origin studies, whether based on fossils or observations of living primates, always carry a risk that some observers will see what they expect to see. Fossil data yield no certain knowledge because the evidence is minimal. Aspects of the past behavior and anatomy of a species have been preserved only accidentally (Tanner 1981:134; Lancaster 1975:3), and some species such as chimpanzees and gorillas left no fossil record because their forested environment precluded the process of fossilization (Zihlman and Tanner 1978:172).

An article in *National Geographic* in 1979 exemplified the misreading of fossil data. In the text, paleontologist Mary Leakey described two sets of footprints set in volcanic ash at Laetoli in Tanzania. The prints were side by side, too close for their makers to have been traveling together. Nonetheless, the illustrator depicted a man with a stick walking directly in front of a woman (Tanner 1981:175).

Observational studies also pose problems. Early field studies accepted as evidence anecdotal tales that still influence social science (Washburn and Hamburg 1965:607). Gathering evidence on creatures in natural surroundings is harder than it seems (Bourliere 1961:1). Merely counting troop members may require hours or days of work, for all individuals are rarely visible at the same time especially among the far more numerous arboreal species. Efforts to recognize individual members often involves insoluble problems, for no one has devised a system of individual marking applicable on a large scale. Many early field studies of monkeys and apes overemphasized the behavior of adult males, who are often larger and more conspicuous than females. Individual primates must be observed equal amounts of time to justify comparative statements (Altmann 1974). Biased observation made it easy to define the social relations of adult males, a small minority, as equivalent to the organization of the entire troop (Lancaster 1975:20).

Interpretation of data also can be difficult. The human mind, quick to generalize, is only too ready to construct an entire social system on the basis of a few observations made in difficult circumstances (Bourliere 1961:2). A species often may be defined as polygynous based on the mere discovery of a group formed of a male and several females, but without proof that the same male was sexually interested in the mature females at estrus. Field workers should avoid terms with precise sociological meaning such as "harem" and use a vocabulary that does not imply a priori the existence of a preconceived social structure.

In the 1960s and 1970s the savanna baboon was widely seen as the best model of the human ancestor. Its ecological situation resembled that of early humans who lived on the open savanna after descending from the trees. The baboon is the most widespread and abundant African primate (Altmann 1998:27), and observing ground-living baboons is far easier than trying to track species that swing from tree to tree in the forest canopy or live in thickets dense and high. The baboon studies readily demonstrate the difficulty of theorizing from a two-sex perspective in a world dominated by the point of view of one sex.

The Baboon Model

Below, I summarize three major studies of baboons that appeared in 1961, 1963, and 1965 in order to convey the substance and flavor of the work that disturbed feminists in the 1970s and 1980s. Conducted by eminent scholars, the studies were widely publicized. In the 1960s no textbook or course in introductory anthropology and no concluding chapter on humans in texts on animal behavior and evolutionary theory was complete without reference to the baboon analogy concerning the lives of early humans. Long after the findings were superseded, they continued to appear in the textbooks of introductory anthropology (Fedigan 1986:39).[2]

Over time, the three studies increasingly depicted females as being dependent on males. The first study rejected the idea of "harems," reported that a "dominant" male is not always dominant, and that females and juveniles are far more likely to go gathering than remain at a "home base." The second one emphasized male defense of females and offspring from predators. The third reported that the largest male monopolized the sexual activities of all adult females and drove away the other males.

In the first study, Washburn and DeVore (1961) compared baboons' daily lives to the presumed lives of the earliest humans. Unlike early humans, adult male baboons were much larger than females, and had huge canine teeth. Group sizes were akin but hunting made early man's range far larger. Nearly vegetarian, baboons lived on small ranges in social systems divided by age, sex, and individual preference. They did not hunt, share, cooperate, or limit sexual activity. Mother-child relations of baboons and early humans were akin but male and female baboons had no lasting social relations or economic ties. At a later period, human males hunted large animals, making human females economically dependent though females and young gathered efficiently. The crucial customs were those that ensured a hunter's services to a woman and her children.

In the second study, based on the same data, DeVore and Washburn (1963) emphasized defense. Adult males defended the troop against dogs or cheetahs though lions put the entire troop to flight.[3] Survival depended on the extent to which the adult males stayed close to other troop members.

The third study (DeVore and Hall 1965) appeared in *Primate Behavior,* a volume that became a classic for thousands of undergraduates and is still found in universities and on the bookshelves of lawyers, doctors, and business executives for whom it was their first or only exposure to the social behavior of our closest relatives (Smuts et al. 1987:ix). The only females with whom the dominant male had no exclusive relations were sexually immature, and he would drive away the other one or two males in the group.

Baboon organizational forms in Kenya and South Africa were said to derive from a complex dominance pattern among adult males that usually ensured stability and carried the highest probability that the males who were most dominant would also father the most offspring. The authors concluded that the social structure of adult females should be studied in detail over a much longer period than had so far been possible. But when the relational pattern of female baboons was worked out, it differed markedly from this account (Smuts 1985).

Man the Hunter

Later in the 1960s, the studies of primatologists began to focus more on the behavior of early humans, especially on the part that hunting had played in human evolution. Washburn and Lancaster's (1968) nearly lyrical paean to the hunting way of life was the most influential and widely quoted expression of models of human evolution in the 1960s. Though the paper was not presented at the symposium that Richard Lee and Irven DeVore convened at the University of Chicago at the invitation of anthropologist Sol Tax, it was included in the volume entitled *Man the Hunter* (Lee and DeVore 1968:vii).[4] Its message was clear: Hunting demanded all the qualities of human behavior that separate man from other primates

(Fedigan 1986:32). A male baboon's defense of the troop was transmuted to a love of hunting, killing, and warfare that men enjoyed.[5] Though it is the use of tools that makes hunting possible, hunting is far more than techniques. It is a way of life that has dominated the course of human evolution for hundreds of thousands of years. In a very real sense, the authors said, human intellect, interests, emotions, and basic social life all are evolutionary products of the success of the hunting adaptation. When anthropologists speak of the unity of mankind, they mean that the selection pressures of the hunting and gathering way of life were so successful and so similar that human populations remain fundamentally the same the world over.

A number of human attributes stemmed from the hunting way of life (Washburn and Lancaster 1968). Hunting and butchering of large animals put a maximum premium on male cooperation and involved sharing, technical skills, planning, knowledge of many species and large areas, and a division of labor by sex. Moreover, men enjoy hunting and killing. One motivation for hunting is the immediate pleasure it gives the hunter, as demonstrated by the efforts to maintain killing as a sport. Ignoring a sizable number of claims to the contrary, the authors asserted that war has been far too important in history for it to have been other than pleasurable for those who were involved. Till recently, war was seen much the same way as hunting, though in recent times, the authors said, the wisdom of war as normal national policy has been questioned.

The Hunter Hits the Media

Popular writing about man the hunter exaggerated the findings that had appeared in scholarly journals, sometimes to the point of explicit misogyny. Males were seen as aggressive, competitive, protective; females as dependent, nurturing, and submissive. Like Darwin's phrases that were incorporated into the myth of Social Darwinism, the assumption that males used tools for hunting and warfare became a part of the Western evolutionary myth of human origins that legitimized male involvement in warfare (Tanner 1981:195).

Perhaps the myths of the dominant male baboon and man the hunter that appeared in the 1960s and 1970s were a reaction to the resurgence of feminist currents that had begun to stir in the 1950s, such as de Beauvoir's (1953) analysis of *The Second Sex* and Friedan's (1962) dissection of *The Feminine Mystique* a little later, which Tiger (1969:72) cited. Popular accounts of baboons and men read as if they had been devised as a cautionary tale directed to women lest they be getting funny ideas about their proper place. The message was clear. Nature designed men to make war, protect women and juveniles, and take charge of affairs. Women belonged at home with the kiddies.

Four writers exemplify the popular marketing of man the hunter: dramatist Robert Ardrey, zoologist Desmond Morris, political sociologist Lionel Tiger, and anthropologist Robin Fox. Below, I summarize their work in order to enable contemporary scholars better to understand why feminists so fiercely rejected biology.

Ardrey's *African Genesis* appeared in 1961. A 1930 zoology graduate from the University of Chicago, then a dramatist of some repute, Ardrey claimed that paleontologist Raymond Dart had been correct. Early man could evolve from an anthropoid background for one reason only: He had become a killer. For our ancestral killer ape, the rock he held meant the margin of survival, for it put new demands on his nervous system that resulted in a bigger brain. Man did not father the weapon; the weapon fathered man. Man takes more delight in his weapons than his women (Ardrey 1961:21, 204). Thus was the myth of the killer ape born, including the link between warfare and hunting and the idea that aggression drives cultural progress (de Waal 2001:45).[6]

Zoologist Desmond Morris (1967) began *The Naked Ape* by scolding anthropologists for rushing to "unsuccessful cultural backwaters" to gather the data to unravel basic truths about human nature. Scholars might as well ignore backward societies that are not in the biological mainstream of evolution because the only sound biological approach is to examine behavioral patterns shared by successful members of major cultures. These persons are the ones who have been influenced heavily by a long evolutionary history. (Most anthropologists would probably disagree with this claim.)

In order to improve his brain, the naked ape took up hunting while the women stayed at the home base owing to the long period of juvenile dependency. As sex roles became more distinct, hunting parties became all male. The development of the pair bond ensured male support of females, who could then devote themselves to maternal duties. The men could be certain of the loyalty of their women, and could therefore avoid fighting over them and could also leave them in order to go hunting. Ardrey says that the process to assure this outcome was never perfected though he does not explain why.

Lionel Tiger, a 1962 PhD in political sociology, London School of Economics and Political Science, published *Men in Groups* in 1969. He hypothesized that human male behavior reflected a biological propensity rooted in evolutionary history. Specialization for hunting programmed the male-male link for hunting and killing and the female-offspring link for feeding and rearing children into the life course of each sex. Women are normally pregnant or nursing nearly all of the time (Tiger 1969:45).

Had he stopped here, Tiger's explanation as to why women took no part in hunting and warfare would be akin to my own (save for his ignoring the effect of technology on fertility and lactation) but he expanded the argument in an amazing fashion: Few women have ever taken part in politics because all women suffer relatively "rigid disabilities" that preclude their access to a public forum. Women simply may not provide the "releasers" or satisfactory images of power and foresight that induce groups to follow leaders (Tiger 1969:204ff). Solicitous of a sex burdened with so onerous a condition, Tiger adds that a woman entrusted with huge responsibilities would be biologically bewildered at being unable to assimilate the stimuli that evolution requires for decisionmaking on social order and defense. A polity even partly dominated by females may go well beyond the limits of healthy possibilities.

The effects of male bonding in new towns and suburbs must also be studied. Men need haunts that exclude women, a place that is not only all male but also antifemale. Tiger (1969:208) hopes that no one will think he implies any hostility between the sexes, for he wants only to energize men constructively in order that they may counterbalance the heavy emotional demands that twentieth century family life makes on men.

In 1965, Lionel Tiger met Robin Fox at a symposium of the Royal Society held at the London Zoo (Tiger and Fox 1971: x). In their first book, *The Imperial Animal,* they claimed that the social system of baboons demonstrates how evolution affects human lives today. Males dominate the political system; dominant males keep order among females and young. Females nurture offspring, staying near the big males, who usually drive off leopards and lions when the troop crosses the savanna. Mature males defend and control the group (Tiger and Fox 1971:32, 29, 86). Thus, war, fighting, and hunting are the business of human males as troop protection is the business of male baboons. Male domination of the political arena from tribe to empire taps the biological basis of the behavior. Women disrupt the unity, loyalty, and trust needed by comrades at arms (Tiger and Fox 1971:57, 98). The male primate who dominates and protects the troop plays politics with some males and forms alliances with others but he always dominates his females, for men hunted and made war. Women did not.[7]

Politics must have seemed hopelessly bizarre to females and frighteningly irrelevant to the simple concerns of their constituents: their children (Tiger and Fox 1971:100). Coeducation at the college or university level is always a mistake: To pretend that boys and girls aged 15 to 21 are substitutable one for the other denies not only biological reality but the entire course of evolution (Tiger and Fox 1971:173).

Woman the Gatherer

Because of the failure to consider females in devising human evolutionary models, the model of man the hunter created a backlash against sexism that was centuries overdue in the study of humanity (Stanford 2001:108). To my knowledge, the first attempt to point to problems with the male model of human origins was Sally Linton's (1971) essay on male bias in anthropology that originally appeared in Suellen Jacobs' cross-cultural study guide. Only a biased theory, Linton said, would claim that males alone developed skills, learned to cooperate, invented language and art, and created tools and weapons while dependent females stayed home having babies. Modern forager women provide the major portion of the diet and there is no reason to assume that this was untrue of early humans.

During the 1970s new research suggested that it was not male hunting parties but females and offspring who were critical to ape-human divergence because, together, they had invented a technology of gathering. The children most likely to survive were born to mothers who were the best gatherers, the most effective tool users, and who walked or carried burdens most efficiently and shared gathered food with their children (Tanner 1981:268; see also Tanner and Zihlman 1976; Zihlman 1978). Contrary to the assumptions underlying the hunter model, neither upright walking nor weapons are needed for chimpanzee, baboon, or early hominid predation, which reduces the likelihood that predator behavior and meat eating were the new elements in hominid origins (Zihlman and Tanner 1978:171).

The new pattern in hominid behavior and basis of human divergence from ancestral apes was the bipedal gathering of plant food (Zihlman and Tanner 1978:175–81). Bipedal locomotion evolved to enable humans to cover long distances while simultaneously carrying food to share, digging sticks, objects for defense, and offspring. Earlier models had proposed that bipedalism emerged to improve hunting activities, but endurance for long distance walking does not vary by sex. Hominid mothers probably gathered food often because the survival of their offspring depended on it. The high drama of man the hunter disappeared. Heroic qualities rarely are needed to obtain protein from catfish, termites, snails, gerbils, and baby baboons (Dahlberg 1981:27).

The hunting of large animals is a high risk but low return activity. The precise skills and refined tools it requires likely became common only after the gathering of nuts and berries provided a nutritional base to enable the hunters to expend energy on activities of uncertain success (Zihlman and Tanner 1978:185). This mode of hunting probably emerged only 500,000 years ago, long after apes and humans diverged. Meat may have become a critical food source only after hominids migrated from Africa into Eurasia where plant growth is seasonal. Meat consumption varies with latitude: at the equator, 10 percent of the forager diet is meat; in the Arctic where few plants grow, 90 percent (Testart 1988).

A Model of Man the Gatherer

The idea that women's gathering might be the basis of human divergence from the apes took an unexpected turn in 1981 in an invited article in the prestigious journal *Science.* Fedigan's (1986) devastating rebuttal of the arguments appeared later in the esteemed *Annual Review of Anthropology.* Citing none of the research on woman the gatherer, physical anthropologist Owen Lovejoy explained that the origin of man was based on a male activity, but not the killing of animals. Lovejoy (1981:348) claimed that no evidence showed that early hominids hunted. Instead, the Australopithecine male became bipedal in the process of gathering food to supply his four-footed mate and his offspring. The stimulus for male gathering was the mortality rate suffered by mothers and infants in the search for food. Thinking that early hominids were on the brink of extinction, Lovejoy hoped to identify an aspect of bipedalism that would explain why it increased the number of living offspring (Falk

1992:91). The greater seasonality of the Miocene plus the need to increase infant survivorship favored some separation of male and female food ranges. Females could stay home, Lovejoy reasoned, if males did not compete for local foods. Unlike birds and canids that can carry food in their mouths or regurgitate sizable amounts, oral carrying of food would have been inadequate for humans, but a strong selection for bipedal locomotion would allow males to carry provisions by hand. Monogamous pair bonding would select for Lovejoy's proposed feeding strategy.

Thus, the anatomical characteristics that could reinforce pair bonds would be under strong positive selection. The human male develops body and facial hair and a conspicuous penis. The human female becomes sexually receptive on a continuous basis and develops prominent and permanently enlarged mammae, unlike the breasts of other female primates that enlarge only during lactation. Lovejoy concluded that both an advanced material culture and an accelerated brain development followed an already-established system of hominid characteristics that included intensified parenting and social relationships, monogamous pair bonding, specialized sexual and reproductive behaviors, as well as bipedal locomotion. The nuclear family and human sexual behavior that contributed to it may have originated long before the dawn of the Pleistocene.

Yet, even in 1981 when Lovejoy's thesis appeared, a number of published studies had shown that female monkeys and apes as well as women foragers remain mobile in all stages of reproduction (Zihlman 1997:102) and the much-publicized idea of monogamy among the earliest humans now seems far-fetched (Wrangham 2001:134–5). Male australopithecines were about twice as large as females. The disparity in size implied that selection favored male fighting ability, for it is well known that monogamy yields little benefit to males who fight one another.

Other obstacles to Lovejoy's theory include skepticism that a male who left his mate to find food for her could guard her effectively from rival males, the absence of evidence for home bases, and the question as to what ultimately induced Lovejoy's four-footed females to become bipedal. Yet, Lovejoy's theory long represented orthodoxy about human evolution (Fedigan 1986:37) and, despite much evidence to the contrary, the thesis was widely invoked long after its publication (Falk 1997:116).

A powerful conceptual model for reconstructing hominid evolution does not yet exist in well-developed form (Tooby and DeVore 1987:190). To be complete and accurate, such a model would have to describe the special adaptations of each age and sex class and the relation of each to the others. Any account of hominid evolution that concentrates on one sex or suggests that any specific age-sex class brought about hominid evolution is deficient per se (Binford 1989:286).

Unresolved Issues

Many issues concerning the origin of human behavior remain unresolved. There is no mainstream view on the topic of human evolution (de Waal 2001a:6). The most accurate reconstruction of our past likely will be based on a broad comparison of bonobos, chimpanzees, and humans within a larger evolutionary context. We are related as closely to one species as to the other. Chimpanzees are male dominated. Bonobos are female dominated. The current issue is not which species is closer to us but rather which one is more like the last common ancestor (de Waal 2001b:41ff). Despite passionate claims both ways, the matter is far from settled.

A society modeled on chimpanzees tends to support a male-biased evolutionary scenario much more than one based on the less well known bonobo. Only late in the 1990s did many strands of knowledge come together concerning this female-centered and relatively peaceful anthropoid ape. Bonobos long remained obscure because their eroticism tended to embarrass scientists. General journals used euphemisms like "very affectionate" to describe bonobo sexual behavior, and some scientists ignored activities with same-sex partners, but once the news about their sex life hit the popular press, bonobo eroticism became an advantage (de Waal 2001b:62). Sex is part of their social life in every partner combination: male-male, male-female, female-female, male-juvenile, female-juvenile.[8] Easily aroused, bonobos use every position and variation and then some. Their societies are usually described as female dominated.

An adequate theory of human evolution needs to take account of the three major characteristics that mark human societies: male bonding, female bonding, and the nuclear family. We share male bonding with chimpanzees; female bonding, with bonobos. We share the nuclear family form with neither ape species (de Waal 2001b:62). Humans have been adapted for millions of years to a social order revolving around reproductive units for which no parallel exists among any nonhuman primate.

The critical question in the evolution of human social structure is to explain why both males and females have foregone the high rates of promiscuity that characterize chimpanzees and bonobos to settle for pair bonding on a more or less long-term basis (Pusey 2001:35–6). Until recently, most scholars thought that pair bonds evolved to facilitate the exchange of resources between the sexes owing to the long dependency of infants and juveniles (see Chapter 3). An alternative hypothesis now attracts growing support: A steady mate protects a female against sexual coercion by other males.

The evolutionary reason for male sexual coercion among nonhuman primates became clear only in the early 1980s after Sarah Blaffer Hrdy (1979) analyzed the accounts of female sexual and reproductive strategies (Strier 2001:88; Lee 1996:27). A female primate's offspring was at risk of being killed by a "foreign" male whose fitness would benefit if an offspring sired by an unrelated competitor were replaced with one of his own. Killing the female's nursling stopped lactation and induced the return of ovulation so that she would soon mate with the "foreign" male. Few primate females limit themselves to a single mate, for it is prudent for a female primate to confuse her infant's paternity.

The wealth of new data on social patterns within and among free-living primates suggest that new questions about female mate choice and male sexual coercion are now coupled with new methods to determine paternity. Pereira, Clutton-Brock, and Kappeler (2000:271), whose account I follow, note that most male mammals desert females after mating and seek other females, but male primates tend to associate permanently with at least one female, and many primates form groups with many males and females. Continuous sexual access was initially suspected as the reason for these groups, but predictable periods of female fertility make this unlikely.

The factor now seen to have the most potential to explain male-female association is male protection of a female from the sexual coercion of other males. Male coercion is widespread in primates. Infanticide is one tactic. Females who carry their infants rather than "parking" them are very vulnerable, and this behavior predicts the rate of lasting male-female association in primates. In many primates, variable social relations within or between sexes can be explained only with data on female reproductive tactics.

Females use a variety of behavioral and physiological mechanisms to choose mates: precopulative tactics that reduce male harassment, defensive coalitions with other females, synchronization and concealment of fertile periods, and timing migration to minimize the risk of infanticide. The most important mechanism may be so-called cryptic female choice that occurs after the coupling of genitalia, and affects male reproductive success (Pereira, Clutton-Brock, Kappeler 2000:274). The selection is cryptic in that assessing male reproductive success by counting copulations with potentially fertile females will not detect it. Neither mounting with pelvic thrusting nor ejaculation indicates that a given male has sired an infant born at an appropriate later date, for few ejaculations result in fertilization. Instead, physiological and anatomical processes under female control determine whether a given male is likely to sire a female's next infant.

However, postcopulatory (cryptic) female control of paternity has received little attention in animal behavior and almost none in primatology. It is most likely to evolve when a male coerces female copulation. Primates whose females typically mate with more than one male have the most anatomical and behavioral evidence of cryptic choice, which selectively favors paternity by conspecific males with a particular trait over males who lack the trait when the female has copulated with both types (Eberhard 1996:8).

In sum, in the 1960s the baboon model suggested that male dominance was natural in humans. Dominant primates were male, the dominant male fathered the most offspring, and man the hunter exemplified all that was finest in human life. Feminists cringed. Yet in the 1970s many of them, some reluctantly, agreed that gender was merely a social construction that could change with the fluctuations in cultural arrangements. Though Brown's (1970:1075) analysis of the gendered division of labor among foragers and horticulturists made it clear that childrearing had never been a primary male obligation, scholars in both cultural anthropology and sociology simply stopped asking why.

Notes

1. Hrdy (1981) exemplified the undoing of masculinist dogma (di Leonardo 1998:268).

2. The baboon model was abandoned only when it became clear that chimpanzees exhibit basic human traits that are absent or undeveloped in baboons: cooperative hunting, tool use, food sharing, power politics, and primitive warfare. An aspect of evolution left unchanged when the chimpanzee became the model of choice was male superiority, which was discredited later with the discovery of the bonobo (de Waal 2001:45, 48).

3. After following three troops for five years, Rowell (1972:44) never saw baboon males defend a troop. Baboons react to danger by flight, males first; females with the biggest infants, last. Protective male behavior against less threatening predators may be due more to low vulnerability than high motivation to defend the group (Cheney and Wrangham 1987:227). Stuart Altmann (1979) concluded that baboon flight behavior is random.

4. Ironically, the symposium on man the hunter provided the data that led to its undoing (Fedigan 1986:34). Lee's (1968) paper "What Hunters Do for a Living" reported that hunters gather more than hunt.

5. A more recent view of early hominids holds that they were not the bold big-game hunters that Raymond Dart and Sherwood Washburn imagined. Instead, they hunted small animals and took meat from carnivores by driving them away from kills (Stanford 2001:105).

6. Konrad Lorenz's (1963) book on aggression claimed that humans endanger one another because the species lacked time to evolve the inhibitions of "professional" killers like lions.

7. That men cannot feed infants the only food they can digest explains why only men hunt and wage war. There is no need to posit a division of labor based on male killer instinct and female inability to make decisions on social order and defense (Lancaster 1975:79).

8. Bonobo males can have a penile erection at about six months, but the very small external genitalia of females encourage genital-genital rubbing only after they are about six years old and close to adolescence (Kano and Vineberg 1992:197).

Chapter Three

The Hominids Appear

MOST OF US ARE AWARE that rearing a child necessarily focuses on resource allocation. Mothers have always had to apportion survival needs such as food, clothing, and shelter (to say nothing of emotional support) between themselves, the children they have, and those who may be born later. The investment of time, energy, and resources in one child lessens a mother's ability to invest in her other children and her ability to produce more of them. With frequent and insistent demands, an infant can even try to extract more investment than any parent has been selected to give (Trivers 1992). The conflicts that employed mothers confront are not new (Hrdy 1992:409). Human motherhood always required compromise between maternal subsistence needs and the time, energy, and resources needed to mate and rear offspring.

It is less well known that natural selection deepened the already lopsided gendering of primate parenthood by ensuring that human mothers would invest far more time and energy in offspring than did other primate mothers. A bigger brain resulted in a painful and risky delivery of an essentially premature infant. In this chapter, I first compare natural selection and cultural change then discuss the trade-offs by which natural selection offset huge benefits with some heavy costs.

Natural Selection and Cultural Change

The human condition is a consequence of the interaction of natural selection, measured in eons for our species, and cultural change, which now seems to happen almost overnight. An environment to which humans adapted over a very long period may change so rapidly owing to the advent of new technologies that the costs can be totally unexpected. For example, during the period of rapidly rising affluence during the 1950s in the so-called First World, no one expected that half a century later the planet would lack the resources to bring Third World countries up to First World standards. Hard choices are in the offing. The values to which most people inappropriately cling when times get hard are those that were once the source of their greatest triumphs over adversity (Diamond 2005:495, 275).

Natural selection, based on the tendency of all living organisms to produce more offspring than can survive, occurs at a slow pace. Offspring vary randomly among themselves, and some of the variation is passed on to future generations. Survivors tend to be individuals whose variations happen to be those that are best suited to an ever-changing local environment (Gould 1996:138). It is the accumulation of favorable variants over time that produces evolutionary change. After random variation provides the raw material of change, natural selection eliminates most of the variations and preserves those individuals fortuitously adapted to a particular local environment. However, if a gene presents a strong selective advantage, it can be spread by natural selection in only a few hundred or a few thousand years (Cavalli-Sforza 2000:45).

Smuts (1995:4) has explained why it is important to avoid the common error that evolutionary adaptation implies genetic determinism. Far from being "fixed" traits, many adaptations, especially behavioral ones, are exquisitely sensitive to environmental variation. Humans are extremely sensitive to both past experience and present environment, for natural selection favored the evolution of brains specialized to respond flexibly to the extremely diverse and variable conditions in which humans live. The idea that a behavior can be biologically adaptive yet environmentally determined is hard to grasp because American culture is so deeply permeated by erroneously dichotomous ways of thinking about genes and behavior.

At the individual level, the random degeneration of natural selection's complex adaptive system is called senescence. The end of the reproductive period cancels the need for more programming of the machinery selected for that purpose. Which component fails first or fastest depends on individual luck in having a genetic endowment viable in a particular setting and culture (Crews 2003:51). Degenerative diseases most often occur in those who survive their fourth decade, a very small segment 300 years ago. The current "epidemic" may be due partly to the number of people living well beyond 40 years and to improved medical diagnosis (Crews and James 1991:186).

Once a species separates from an ancestral line, it remains forever distinct. Species do not amalgamate with one another, for a species consists only of individuals who are capable of interbreeding and producing fertile offspring under natural conditions. Sexual reproduction limits an individual to contributing only half of his or her genes to the next generation, but it enhances the probability that at least some of those genes will survive environmental change.

Compared to the speed of social change, natural selection proceeds like a tortoise whose gait varies from several hundreds to millions of years. Five or six million years ago after our hominid ancestors split off from a common ancestor with the chimpanzees (Trivers 1985:388), posture and locomotion became features of a single kind of adaptation that marks the beginning of the hominid lineage. Our omnivorous primate ancestors who moved to the edge of the forest began to include part of the grasslands in their foraging (Kelso and Trevathan 1984:104).

Though hominids had been around millions of years, anatomically modern humans (the subspecies Homo sapiens sapiens) emerged in East and South Africa about 150,000 years ago (Turner and Maryanski 2005:84). Wolpoff (1992) is skeptical about a solely African origin, but majority opinion now holds that our ancestors were Africans who spread to the rest of the world in the past 100,000 years, first to Asia then to its appendices, Oceania, Europe, and America (Cavalli-Sforza 2000:85).

Homo sapiens sapiens differed from earlier humans, including the well known Neanderthals. More robust than modern humans, the Neanderthals developed in Europe from the early human ancestor. For a long time they were the only human type living in Europe and parts of the Near East. Their brains were larger than ours though there is no strong archeological evidence that their behavior was more advanced. Their disappearance from various parts of Europe 40,000 to 30,000 years ago coincided with the appearance of modern humans (Cavalli-Sforza et al. 1994:62). On occasion, an imaginative writer supplies a scenario that describes how our kind did the Neanderthals in, but no one really knows why they disappeared.

The variation between any human populations thus far identified is far less than the variation within a given population (Ruvulo 1997:536), but the effect of a given ecology upon superficial physical attributes has been strong enough to allow various populations to be identified statistically from one another (Cavalli-Sforza 2000). For example, skin color changed as peoples moved to northern latitudes. Dark color, the original shade of our species, originally evolved as a defense against too much ultraviolet radiation. Skin color is darkest in hot, dry areas to protect against cancer and lightest at high latitudes to permit production of vitamin D for bone growth (Cavalli-Sforza et al. 1994:266). Females are lighter than males in all of the populations studied (Jablonski 2004:585, 601).

It is sobering that our species is the only one in the hominid line that has not become extinct. Though we humans like to see ourselves as the final link in the great chain of being (Lovejoy 1957), evolution does not imply progress (Granovetter

1979; Lenski 2005). Our species is the product of evolution, not the purpose (Wilson 1998:31). The evolutionary successes in the mammal line (many species, vigorous radiation) are bats, rats, and antelopes (Gould 1996:63).

For a long time after the appearance of modern humans, the pace of social change was nearly imperceptible. Thus, for about 99 percent of human history, our ancestors hunted and gathered to obtain their food. The rate of change quickened after the first great cultural revolution in human history, the invention of agriculture about 10,000 years ago. The great empires and kingdoms of Eurasia began to appear only a few thousand years after our ancestors began to domesticate plants and animals. In contrast to species evolution, societal development must be explained in terms of our genetic heritage, technologies, and the resources and constraints not only of the biophysical environment but also of the sociocultural environment and the impact of intersocietal selection (Lenski 2005:7).

After the plow became the modal tool used to produce food across most of Eurasia, the pattern of social stratification assumed a pyramidal shape. At the tip of the pyramid, an elite composed of warrior kings and their minions rested on a thin layer of artisans, merchants, and priests. The base was comprised of a mass of peasants, serfs, and slaves, an unlucky bunch any way you look at it (Huber 1999). Nonetheless, because there were so many of them, they comprise nearly all of the ancestors of contemporary humans.

Most of the benefits of the plow mode of stratification went to the rich and powerful. The costs were borne by the poor and powerless, who often got too little to eat in a diet predominantly based on grain. Peasants, serfs, and slaves and even knights and princes became shorter in stature than their forager ancestors, who had been as tall as contemporary Westerners. Then, probably because the discovery and conquest of the New World had so enriched the countries of the so-called West and stimulated technological innovation and the rise of science (Lenski 2005:178), a little less than 300 years ago the stirrings of an incipient industrial revolution initiated sweeping change in behavior and belief systems across the European peninsula. It was a case of the more, the more as the pace of change quickened. The discomfiting awareness of having become passé in a changed world seizes the imagination of each generation in turn. Though our parents, grandparents, and great-grandparents endured such transitions (and certainly spoke of them often enough), we are just as astonished as they were that everyday reality can change so fast. The structure of human consciousness apparently makes it easy for us to see ourselves as the unchanging center of a stable universe.

A mechanism unknown in the slow world of Darwinian evolution powers cultural change: the explosively fruitful or devastatingly destructive impact of the shared traditions that humans develop in response to changes in their environment (Gould 1996:220). The effects of science and technology often elicit unanticipated moral problems nowhere more clearly than in the area of human reproduction. The biblical injunction to be fruitful and multiply was once a good road map for our species. Now the problem is to recognize when enough is enough.

Two-Sex Trade-Offs

All change, whether the result of natural selection or human culture, tends to involve trading costs that may offset the benefits of change. We tend to be more aware of the trade-offs in cultural change because a given complex of events typically occurs right under our noses. For example, it is no secret that an atom bomb enables a nation-state to pulverize enemies at the risk of being pulverized in return. We tend to be less aware of the trade-offs of natural selection, and we are often unaware of the fact that some trade-offs affect one sex much more than the other. I first describe several trade-offs that affected both sexes. Random variation produces random design, not optimal design from the perspective of the creature involved.

Lower Back Problems

Some costs stem from changes that are only about five million years old. Vertebral arthritis occurred even among prehistoric hunter-gatherers who were on the move most of the time, and is not merely a pathological response to modern lifestyles (Strassman and Dunbar 1999:92). The lower back problems that are induced by bipedal locomotion are exacerbated by the tendency of us moderns to earn a living sitting down, but painful lumbar ailments afflict nearly everyone sooner or later. The best way to avoid lumbar problems is to die young.

Sex and Excrement

Other problems go back very far indeed (Potts and Short 1999:133). We humans enter the world squeezed uncomfortably between the maternal rectum and bladder, jammed between the unyielding walls of the bony pelvis. The problem began about 350 million years ago when our earliest aquatic ancestors took a particular fork in the evolutionary road. The Blind Watchmaker of evolution hijacked a couple of tubes that collected urine from the kidneys and used them to carry eggs and sperm to the watery world outside. This alteration gave humans the opportunity to associate sex with the elimination of waste and also resulted in serious physiological dangers for big-brained land animals hundreds of millions of years later, soon to be addressed in detail.

Language

The study of human languages has produced amazing discoveries in the past 60 years though contentious issues abound (Greenberg 2005). Most scholars agree that the origin is probably biological, too enmeshed with other cognitive abilities to have developed fast and late in human evolution. Language likely appeared when we still lived on the same continent, for all children learn sounds in the same order, p-m-a first, r last (Ruhlen 1994:122). The demands made by increasing group size increased language complexity (Dunbar 1996:115); the complexity of contemporary languages probably appeared about 100,000 years ago (Cavalli-Sforza 2000:93). Today there are 5,000 odd languages (Ruhlen 1987:3) and most of them are only between 25,000 and 5,000 years old (Cavalli-Sforza et al. 1994:155).

The changes that enabled humans to communicate in language stemmed from a series of adaptations that enabled hominids to exploit the resources of the African savanna (Reader 1997:108). Teeth and jaws evolved to deal with available food. We became hairless, like oversized Chihuahuas save for the thatch on top where the African sun beat down directly and the curly fringes in our armpits and around our private parts. The naked skin became part of a body cooling system that permitted early humans to forage in the heat of the day, which, in turn, facilitated the evolution of a large brain (Falk 1992).

Because our primate ancestors had already developed visual dominance (unlike the olfactory dominance in other mammals), they could leap safely, at least most of the time, from tree to tree. Moving to the open savanna presented new problems. Open country offers little refuge; hence most mammals rely on a keen long-distance olfactory sense to detect predators and prey. The primate stereoscopic visual system readily detects the distance of predators in space but vision becomes less useful in dim light and useless in the dark. Thus, when vision is deficient as an early warning organ and the sense of smell is greatly reduced, selection tended to place the auditory-vocal channel under volitional control. Voluntary acoustic sounds first evolved in hominids as a sensory tool to enhance the image construction of an already sophisticated visual system (Maryanski 1996:96). The rewiring that permitted visual dominance selectively advantaged the rewiring of human neuron anatomy to integrate the sensory inputs that made spoken language possible (Turner 2000:21).

Language came at a steep price: We are the only mammals who can choke while eating. No free lunch. About one person in a hundred thousand chokes to death each year, a low rate compared to that from automobile accidents, but a persistent cause of death during all of human evolution, especially for the very old and the very young (Diamond 1992:54). The rearrangement of larynx, tongue, and pharynx that permits human speech also lets food fall into the larynx and cuts off air. Our food-conveying esophagus is located behind the air-conveying trachea in our chest, so the tubes must cross in the throat. If food blocks the intersection, air cannot reach the lungs. After infancy, those who most often incur the cost of our speaking ability are generally too old to reproduce but young enough to consume substances that stimulate conviviality by inducing relaxation. A nicely relaxed epiglottis increases the opportunity to choke.

Sudden Infant Death Syndrome

Until the age of about three months, the human infant has an upper respiratory tract like that of other mammals but unlike that of adult humans. The neonate's tract allows it to swallow and breathe at the same time (Trevathan 1987:135; Lieberman and Blumstein 1988:206). The larynx is located high in the neck close to the nasal cavity such that it allows direct passage of air from the nose to the lungs. The arrangement separates the nasal breathing pathway from the oral swallowing pathway so that breathing and swallowing occur independently and thus can occur at the same time. The infant is a so-called "obligate nose breather."

At the age of about two to four months as the infant matures and begins assuming the upright posture of a habitual bipedal creature, the larynx, tongue, hyoid bone, and pharynx descend in the neck such that the larynx opens into the lower part of the pharynx and the brain is rewired appropriately to reflect this change. The infant must then swallow and breathe separately lest it choke. This new placement of the larynx (the human voice box) coupled with a rewiring job in the brain enables humans beyond early infancy to produce an almost infinite array of sounds as they develop language to communicate with one another.

Some scholars have suggested that the repositioning of the larynx may affect young infants by way of the so-called Sudden Infant Death Syndrome (SIDS). The syndrome is said to occur when a caretaker finds a seemingly healthy infant dead in its crib, suffocated. One suggested cause is that the infant's mother was insufficiently attentive. Another is that an infant should not lie prone (face down) in its crib. Contemporary childcare gurus seemingly accept this explanation without comment, but it was only 50 years ago that well-trained pediatricians advised mothers always to place an infant in a prone rather than supine position lest the difficulty of releasing intestinal gas induce crying instead of sleeping.

Noting that the SIDS rate is as much as ten times higher in cultures in which babies sleep apart from their parents, Nesse and Williams (1994:205) have suggested that the coordination of maternal and infant sleep cycles may lead to intermittent arousals that sustain SIDS-vulnerable babies when their breathing might otherwise cease. The basic problem, the cessation of infant breathing, may be related to the extreme immaturity of the infant's nervous system, which is the price our kind must pay to avoid the danger of the birth of an infant with a skull too large to pass through its mother's pelvis, a topic soon to be discussed.

The infant is at greatest risk of SIDS at two to four months, when the primary reflex patterns present at birth are being replaced by learned behaviors (Trevathan 1987:126). Sudden infant death may reflect faulty changes in the neural control of respiration during a period when the wiring system is in flux (Lieberman 1998:156). The abrupt change from water living to land living (the major impact of birth on mammal young) requires physiological and behavioral solutions to the problems of maintaining the body in a desiccating and thermally variable environment in which food and water are discontinuous. Some response systems that appear at birth such as the use of the lungs are maintained but others such as the grasping reflex diminish in frequency and intensity (Rovee-Collier and Lipsett 1982:176–7). The period of rapid development of neural function is critical. The infant must learn some behaviors in its first few months before the unlearned protective reflexes have diminished to an ineffective level; otherwise it will be inadequately prepared to survive. At issue is neonatal response to the obstruction of its breathing. A normal infant acts defensively should the mother's breast occlude its nose. Covering a baby's nose elicits a cry of rage that escalates until the covering is removed. In a healthy child, the behavioral escalation is failsafe, for it elicits crying and threshing about till the infant finally frees its nose. If a newborn lacks a strong head-and-hand response to respiratory threats, voluntary behaviors that must supplant a congenital response will remain unlearned. Infants without obviously serious disease who succumb to the syndrome tend to be at least mildly deficient in responding to respiratory occlusion or be in some other way behaviorally lethargic. Such infants probably never learned that breathing through the mouth overcomes the disability of a stuffy nose.

Asthma

Sometimes rapid cultural change saddles humans living in a new setting with totally new and unexpected costs. Unknown among foragers, asthmatic respiratory distress is on the rise in modern economies. Respiratory allergies affected less than one percent of people in industrial societies in 1840. Now they affect ten percent. Hay fever was essentially unknown before 1830 in Britain and 1850 in North America, and its incidence in Japan was negligible in 1950 but now affects about a tenth of the population (Nesse and Williams 1994:170).

Asthma is an unanticipated byproduct of the human capacity to develop an immunoglobulin reaction that originally evolved to mitigate the ills of parasitic invasions of the human body by helminthes and nematodes such as intestinal worms. Roundworms and hookworms still plague about two million people across the world, although they are under control in areas where Western medicine prevails.

Nonetheless, the worms have their revenge. Some of the more pleasing attributes of modern life such as well-insulated dwellings, blankets, mattresses, and carpeting encourage the proliferation of dust mites, tiny arthropods who dine on discarded bits of human skin. (We humans shed much more than we think.) Dust mites play a major role in the sharply rising incidence of childhood asthma (Barnes, Armelagos, and Morreale 1999:209–43). In our warm, draft-free houses the tiny creatures enjoy the opportunity to lodge in lush wall-to-wall carpeting, curtains, and, especially, in bedclothes and pillows that generally contain enough bits of human skin for a series of delightful meals. Because our hominid ancestors developed a partial immune reaction to the ravages of kindred parasites, helminthes and nematodes, many moderns react to the wastes of these tiny creatures with respiratory allergies that are made manifest in varying degrees of severity. Dust mites are a great boon to the sales managers of companies that make plastic covers for mattresses and pillows. Unfortunately, no one has yet figured out how to create a cold-climate substitute for warm blankets and thick carpeting in a nicely heated house.

One-Sex Trade-Offs

Two consequences of natural selection are central to the theme of this book because of their effect on women's use of time: bipedal locomotion (walking and running on two feet), which emerged a little more than five million years ago, and the human brain, which increased in size by about two million years ago. The benefits accrued to both sexes but the costs bore more heavily on women. Both sexes tend to experience lower back problems owing to bipedal locomotion, but the total cost is much greater for women because of the increase in birth trauma, which was further increased by the evolution of a larger brain. There is one cost of the evolution of bipedal locomotion and the larger brain that is less well known: Human females must invest far more time and energy in child care than do their nearest primate relatives or any other female mammals.

Bipedalism evolved more than five million years ago when humans began to walk and run instead of brachiating about in the forest canopy as do monkeys and gibbons or walking quadrupedally by day but nesting in trees at night like other apes. The major reason for the change was an accelerated unsteadiness in the African climate. Rising levels of seasonality induced variation in fauna and flora such that the niche our ancestors had occupied for several million years experienced decreased carrying capacity. Our forebears had to find other niches to exploit, and these new niches required change in behavior, anatomy, and physiology (Trevathan 1987:15).

Though almost all primates can stand on their hind limbs, and many occasionally walk bipedally, walking on two feet is the predominant form of locomotion only among humans. Walking is a unique activity during which the body, step by step, teeters on the verge of catastrophe. Only the rhythmic forward movement of one leg and then the other keeps us from falling flat on our faces (Napier 1993 [1967]).

Bipedal locomotion required significant pelvic change. Otherwise, walkers would have had to place their legs too far apart for a good stride, as contemporary humans must do when they try to get about on snowshoes. The male pelvis could accommodate to the needs of bipedal locomotion much more easily than that of the female, which had to be both of a size and shape to permit passage of the head of the infant during the process of giving birth. A happy outcome of the selection for a larger female pelvis was that the male pelvis came to differ enough from the female pelvis that student paleo-anthropologists could learn how to determine skeletal sex in as few as two or three minutes with relatively little error (Birdsell 1975:354). The consequences for the female whose skeleton it once had been were less happy. Her pelvis was larger but not large enough to prevent the kind of serious and permanent injuries in giving birth soon to be discussed. I first discuss the evolutionary process then explain why bipedalism and a larger brain so increased the trauma of human birth.

The evolution of a much larger brain was a necessary step in the evolution of modern humans from the hominid line because the increase set the stage for the development of human communication by means of language and the emergence of human culture. That increase began about two million years ago. By 100,000 to 200,000 years ago, the size of the brain had doubled.

Men's brains are about 10 percent larger than women's, but women's are larger in relation to their body weight and have a higher density of neurons. Men's and women's brains tend to be wired differently, resulting in cognitive diversity. The biggest reported sex difference is the male edge in visual-spatial skills such as mental rotation of geometrical figures (Falk 1997:125). Women apparently have an edge in learning and using languages and their intuitive skills may surpass men's, though this edge could be a survival skill developed under conditions of political inequality.

Suggested reasons for the increase in brain size include warfare, throwing, work, language, tool production, hunting, and social intelligence. Contemporary opinion leans toward seeing the prime mover as the need for the level of social intelligence required for life in a large group (Falk 1992:129). The benefit of living in larger groups is better defense against predators. The cost is more trouble finding food, which forces individuals within a species to compete with one another. Monkeys and apes generally handle these tensions by mutual grooming. Bonobos use sex as a social emollient. By contrast, humans live in very large and complex social groups that outgrew the capacity of grooming to preserve social order. In a very large group, you would be doing nothing but scratching backs all day (Potts and Short 1999:187).

Dunbar (1996:79) suggests that language may have been the social glue that replaced grooming among humans, for speech enables several people to interact at the same time. To this day, the size of a conversation group is limited by auditory machinery. This hypothesis diametrically opposes the conventional idea that language developed in order to help men improve the management of hunting. Language more likely evolved to permit gossip, which is the basis of social analysis.

A larger brain coupled with the greater efficiency of bipedal locomotion contributed heavily to our species' survival and success, for greater dependence on wits and the need for only two limbs in locomotion enabled hominids to control their environments to a much greater extent. The downside of these marvels was the terrible costs they imposed upon the process of childbirth (Trevathan 1987:21) and the burdensome social restrictions on women's activities as a result of remaining in a nearly continuous state of pregnancy or lactation during their most vigorous years.

The Trauma of Human Birth

Probably the most widely recognized consequence of selection for bipedalism and a large brain was a huge increase in the trauma of birth. The trauma initiated by the pelvic changes associated with bipedalism was enormously compounded by the evolution of a large brain that made birth even more difficult and dangerous for both mother and infant. Female great apes go off alone to give birth. Their birthing is easy compared to ours, for the ratio of infant head to maternal pelvis is like that of yolk to white in a boiled egg. In sharp contrast, the head of the human infant fills the pelvic cavity from top to bottom with only tiny slivers of space to spare at each side (see Schultz 1949). Human mothers and infants are more likely to survive the birth process when they have the help of an experienced female. It is no surprise that studies in paleology indicate that among Neanderthal, Upper Paleolithic, and Mesolithic populations, women between the ages of 21 and 30 were more likely than men in that age range to die owing to the hazards of childbirth (Birdsell 1975:353).

For most of human history, one birth in twenty ended in maternal death. In natural or wild settings and in most human populations lacking modern health care and sanitation, women typically did not outlive men (Crews 2003:36). In the United States, the United Kingdom, and many other modern societies, women currently enjoy a five to seven year advantage over men in expectation of life at birth (about 79 years versus about 72 years), but this advantage is of recent origin and characterizes only the most cosmopolitan societies with well developed resources for maternal and child care. After age 70, the female mortality advantage decreases, and at about age 85, male and female mortality rates converge (Crews 2003:107–8).

Troublesome births had marked the evolutionary history of all the higher primates owing to the pelvic size needed for efficient locomotion, the neonate's large body relative to maternal body size, and the comparatively large fetal cranium (Trevathan 1987:22). For marmosets, squirrel monkeys, baboons, and macaques, the passage of the fetal head through the maternal pelvis is a squeeze, and mortality owing to the discrepancy is significant. For example, spontaneous abortions and stillbirths account for about half of all recorded births among squirrel monkeys (Leutenegger 1981:90). The problem was resolved rather neatly for the great apes after early humans split off from the pongid line because the pongid strategy for birth involved larger adult body size with no increase in neonatal size. A large pelvis in a large body and a relatively small infant made for an easy birth for such pongids as bonobos, chimpanzees, and gorillas. Among contemporary primates, it is primarily human females and some monkeys who share a tendency to experience births that endanger both mother and infant.

The human strategy for birth emerged after the brain had greatly increased in size. Two million years ago the hominid brain reached the maximum size that could be born to a mammal adapted to deliver an infant whose brain is half of its adult size at birth (Trevathan 1987:223). The problem of a further increase in brain size (which made the head too large for safe delivery) was solved not by enlarging the birth canal or the total size of the adult female (as happened among the great apes) but rather by having the birth occur before the infant's brain became too large for safe passage. At birth, a human infant's brain is relatively smaller in proportion to its adult size than in any closely related primate: 23 percent of adult size in a human compared to 45 percent in the chimpanzee and 68 percent in the rhesus monkey. In six or seven months the human brain has grown to 45 percent of adult size. By the fourth year, it is 95 percent of adult size, the usual age of weaning among foragers (Lancaster 1985:20). Thus, during the first few years of life the human brain roughly triples in size, consuming almost half of the infant's resting caloric requirements (Flinn 1999:106).

The passage through the bony maternal pelvis is the most difficult part of birth for the infant, and even today many newborns have skull deformities resulting from the passage (Birdsell 1975:354). The passage through the vagina and other soft tissues poses the greatest hazards to the mother. Third degree lacerations such as the tearing of tissue from vagina to anus are not uncommon in the absence of an episiotomy (widening the opening by cutting flesh to prevent tearing). Unless these lacerations are properly repaired and treated, disabilities and serious infection can result (Trevathan 1987:27).

In quadrupedal species like monkeys as well as in the probable quadrupedal ancestor of humans the entrance and exit of the birth canals have their greatest breadth from front to back. The infant's head is also largest front to back. The head passes straight through the birth canal and the baby monkey emerges facing toward the front of the mother's body. She can reach down with her hands and guide it from the birth canal or it can crawl up toward her nipples unassisted.

By contrast, the evolution of bipedalism twisted the human birth canal in the middle so that the entrance is broadest side to side while the exit is broadest front to back. The widest breadths of entrance and exit are perpendicular to one another as are the relevant fetal dimensions: the head is largest front to back; the rigid shoulders are broadest side to side. The Blind Watchmaker would have won no accolades for Intelligent Design. The passage of the infant's broad, rigid shoulders through the mother's deep bony pelvis requires that the infant's chin be pressed against its throat instead of tilted backwards or extended, like the monkey's. The coupling of this flexion with the restructured bony birth canal requires that the human infant undergo a series of rotations to pass through the birth canal without hindrance (Stoller 1995).

As a result of these rotations the infant tends to be born facing away from its mother. This change is the one that had the greatest impact in transforming birth from a solitary to a social event (Trevathan 1999:195). The infant's facing away hinders the mother's ability to reach down and clear a breathing passageway for it or to remove the cord from around its neck should the cord be interfering with breathing or continued emergence. In most deliveries, if the mother tries to guide the infant from the birth canal, she risks pulling its head backwards, which may damage nerves and muscles. The fix that the infant is in can be simulated by following these simple directions: Lie prone on a couch, then let yourself be maneuvered into a supine position by having someone lift your head, bend it backwards, and (assuming your someone is extremely strong and you are remarkably supple) pull your body after the head.

Thus, the increased size of the brain made the already taut fit between the head of the infant and the maternal pelvis even tighter. One compromise between the larger brain size and narrow birth canal was to delay much more of the brain's growth to the postnatal period. The birth of an infant that was relatively unable to help itself added to the advantage of having another person present to help both mother and infant at the delivery (Trevathan 1999:197).

According to Trevathan (1999), the evolution of bipedalism increased the risks of mortality from unattended birth well above the risks of having other females of one's species in the vicinity, a circumstance that other primate females sought to avoid. Early hominid females who sought assistance during delivery probably had more surviving and healthier offspring than those who continued the ancient mammal pattern of delivering alone. The evolutionary process thus transformed birth from an individual to a social enterprise along with the underlying emotions that motivated the behavior to seek companionship. Unfortunately, twentieth century medical practice tended to isolate mothers and subject them to procedures like enemas and pubic shaves that had no scientific basis. The standard lithotomy position (the mother supine, her feet apart in stirrups) was designed to help the birth attendant, not the mother.

More Work for Mother

A second cost of bipedalism and a large brain has received less attention than the trauma of birth. These two adaptations made much more work for human mothers. The infant was in effect born prematurely, in a helpless (altricial) state, and needed much more care for a longer period than did its young primate cousins. The advantages of the adaptation accrued to the offspring. To have a longer period to learn the ways of the world enormously benefited human juveniles of both sexes by comparison with those of other primates.

Until the end of her reproductive period, a typical mother had to carry her youngest child everywhere she went and sleep with it at night for three or four years to boot because her low-fat milk sated the infant's hunger only briefly (see Chapter 4). She gathered nuts, berries, and killed small animals on a daily basis, all of her children in tow, to provide food for them and teach them to provide for themselves when they were almost fully grown. These obligations barred her from a number of activities which, unfortunately, included those that typically contributed the most to male power and prestige.

Feeding Human Juveniles

A monkey or ape mother will let her juvenile share her feeding territory and social status while the juvenile enjoys her protection and learns about food sources and dangers (Lancaster 1985:11). However, the nutritional independence of nonhuman primate juveniles exacted a steep price. As nonhuman primates share no food, a sick or injured one can die of hunger or thirst. Its relatives may show concern but none will respond to its need for nourishment (Lancaster 1991). Between 70 and 90 percent of the infants fail to reach adulthood owing to malnutrition and the diseases that follow weaning (Lancaster and Lancaster 1983). Moreover, small and weak juveniles are poorly equipped to compete with larger and wilier adults in finding and processing food (Lancaster 1985:12). For nonhuman primates, as for most mammals, the juvenile phase is a selection funnel into which many enter but few emerge (Lancaster 1991).

By contrast, humans are the only mammals whose juveniles do not have to feed themselves (Lancaster 1991). The expansion of the juvenile phase of life came at the cost of increased investment in offspring by parents or closely related adults. Prolonging the period of nutritional dependence doubled the time humans spent in the most perilous part of the life course for carnivores and nonhuman primates that hunt in groups. The protection of human juveniles resulted in a much higher survival rate. About half of the infants born to hunters and gatherers and horticulturists lived long enough to reproduce.

The lengthy period of feeding juveniles and the increasing strength of adult male-female bonds clearly were involved in the emergence of the human family, an arrangement that at minimum includes an adult female and male and some children. Exactly how the arrangement came into being by way of evolution is not as clear as one would like and may never be quite transparent. Lancaster (1991) held that it was male-female collaboration in feeding human juveniles that led to a family of at least one male, one female, a nursing infant, and nutritionally dependent juveniles of various ages. Kaplan and Lancaster (2003:179) recently argued that it was male hunting of large animals that led to the formation of the human family by promoting male-female cooperation and high levels of male parental investment, which in turn facilitated the feeding of juveniles and lowered their mortality while the nutritional dependence of multiple young favored sequential mating with the same person. Citing Kaplan et al. (2001), the authors claimed that forager men provided an average of 97 percent of the calories for offspring; women provided only 3 percent in the only ten societies for which quantitative data on adult food production were said to be available. This claim, which seems high, will doubtless be assessed in future research.

Whether the formation of male-female bonds in humans is the result of male help in feeding juveniles, the protection of the female against the predations of other males as the authors cited in Chapter 2 suggested, or other combinations of activities and emotions remains an open question, for some of the needed data are neurological and have yet to be reported in detail. The best analysis I have seen of the complex of variables most likely involved in the transition from ape communities to human societies is a recent study of the biocultural factors involved in the incest taboo. Turner and Maryanski (2005) argued that the origin of the human family is likely a result of neurological changes that enabled humans to develop forms of organization more tightly knit than were those in other ape communities. The communities of nonhuman primates are characterized by weak ties among adults, high levels of individualism, and mobility among loosely organized foraging parties. This organizational mode did not enhance survival when early hominids left the forest for the savanna where a relatively tight-knit group could better forage and fight off predators. If hominids were to survive, they had to become better organized.

Natural selection acted on the human brain's subcortical regions and the neuronets that connect the neocortex to the limbic systems that generate our emotions, including those that surround sexual unions. However, the strengthening of the conjugal bonds between males and females who shared the rearing of offspring increased the potential for inbreeding. The nuclear family and the incest taboo are interwoven, as all the early theorists on the family recognized. Turner and Maryanski (2005:183) reason that the nuclear family was made possible by the heightening of the emotions, especially those revolving around sex, and perhaps also the sexual division of labor and the ensuing exchange relationship. Male and female bonding for longer periods, the exchanging of meat and plant foods, and sharing in childrearing is unnatural for an ape, but it became a way to raise the fitness of human hunters and gatherers.

Chapter Four

Human Milk

THIS CHAPTER ADDRESSES the causes and consequences of the transition from the frequent and prolonged mode of breastfeeding that persisted until late in the nineteenth century to the variety of contemporary practices that range from feeding an infant only by bottle to feeding only from the breast, with various combinations of bottle and breast in periods of varied length between feeds and with varying amounts of supplementary food. As noted earlier, contemporary breastfeeding today differs substantially from the ancient mode. The intervals between feeds tend to be much longer during the day than formerly and the mother need not keep the infant constantly nearby during the day or routinely sleep with it at night.

After presenting a brief historical background, I discuss the physiology of lactation, the composition of human milk, the discovery of the effect of lactation on ovulation (natural fertility) in the last third of the twentieth century, and the physiological benefits and costs of breastfeeding both to the infant and to the mother.

Historical Background

Until very recently, nearly all babies were breastfed for several years lest they die because human milk was the only food an infant could digest. The physiological consequences of frequent and prolonged breastfeeding were highly beneficial to both mother and child. The social consequences benefited the infant but were on the whole quite negative for the mother, for the practice barred her from the activities that were typically rewarded with the most prestige and power in any society.

Infant diet was affected by subsistence technology. Among hunter-gatherers, there were no good alternatives to human milk for infant nourishment. The foods consumed by older children and adults were too tough and hard to chew and digest to be given to infants or young children whose little guts and teeth had not matured enough to enable them to process such items as incompletely ripened fruit, nuts, insects, and small animals. After foragers learned to use fire, they cooked vegetable tubers and meats to soften them. Even so, these foods were hard for young children to digest. Hence a mother's need to breastfeed her own child went unquestioned. To leave infant care to other group members was not an option among early hominids, for it was highly unlikely that another lactating woman would be available to serve as a wet nurse (Trevathan 1987:32; Hrdy 1999:402).

The domestication of animals such as cows, sheep, and goats and the invention of settled agriculture 10,000 years ago provided alternatives to breastfeeding in the event of maternal death or disinterest, but the new options were in fact illusory. Giving cow's milk to an infant seemed sensible enough, for many herders drank the milk of the animals they tended. Moreover, milk was so nutritious that adults living in herding societies had adapted physiologically to digesting lactose (milk sugar), unlike all other mammals (including humans) who lost that ability after weaning (Cavalli-Sforza 2000:46). However, cows' milk had far too little sugar to supply the needs of the infant's rapidly growing brain and far too much fat for the infant to digest properly.

The domestication of various grains resulted in the proliferation of more digestible plant foods that needed much less chewing than did the tubers and roots consumed by foragers. From an early age, an infant could swallow a mushy mixture of grain and milk or water. Yet, even though infant pap needed little chewing, it failed to supply the nutrients of human milk. Of more importance, the grain-based diet that was not good for adults (see Chapter 5) was highly dangerous for infants and young children. Stored food provided a good home for the disease pathogens that thrived in the warm climates of West Asia where erstwhile foragers first settled. Absent any knowledge of pathogens and the concomitant prevalence of unsafe drinking water, most of the food that adults ate was contaminated, some of it very badly spoiled. Adults generally developed some immunity to a variety of disease-producing organisms but the immature infant gut, especially in the absence of the immune factors supplied by human milk, was highly vulnerable to pathogens that led to diarrhea and all too often to death from dehydration.

The mode of infant feeding began to change by the end of the nineteenth century in areas in which advances in applied science had altered behavior and public opinion. Scientists discovered ways to kill or neutralize the disease pathogens that flourish in food and water supplies. The techniques spread more slowly than one would have hoped in areas that were already well developed economically and at an even slower pace in the less developed regions where the majority of the world's peoples lived. A recent study reported that the average age of cessation of breastfeeding worldwide was 4.2 years (Hervada and Newman 1992).

Wolf (2001:Chapter 1) argues that it was the mothers themselves who modified the custom of prolonged breastfeeding by exposing infants at younger and younger ages to assorted artificial foods, most of which had cows' milk as a primary, if not sole, ingredient. In turn, the use of supplementary foods reduced the mother's milk supply. By the end of the nineteenth century, maternal complaints about inadequate amounts of breast milk induced physicians in the new specialty of pediatrics to attend to the appropriate feeding of infants. Some notions seem odd, like the fear of overfeeding fueled by an obsession with intestinal regularity: In 1913 the Chicago

Department of Health warned that overfeeding killed hundreds of babies (Wolf 2001:36).

Worry about the contamination of urban milk supplies spurred the development of an "artificial" infant food industry that permitted more infants to survive without breastfeeding than in any earlier period of history, but not until the mid-twentieth century did these products begin to be widely used (Stuart-Macadam 1995:26, 28). In the western world, infant formula began to replace human milk from about the 1950s, beginning earlier where standards of public sanitation and female education were relatively high. The transition continues across those parts of the world that are now in the process of developing more modern economies.

In effect, the introduction of a relatively safe mode of bottle feeding comprised a revolution for it soon resulted in huge behavioral consequences, beginning with a sizable reduction in the numbers of mothers who breast-fed at all (Stuart-Macadam 1998:58). The most significant change by far was the decrease to nearly zero in the number of three-to-five-year-old children whose primary food was human milk. A pattern that characterized our species from the beginning disappeared in about a century. In the United States, for example, unrestricted breastfeeding was dominant early in the twentieth century. An infant was given the breast whenever it cried or fussed, leading to many feedings a day. Today, token breastfeeding prevails. Unlimited suckling is out. The clock determines the frequency and duration of most infant feedings. Weaning usually occurs in the third month or earlier (Lawrence and Lawrence 1999:203). It was for good reason that the World Health Organization (1981) described artificial infant feeding as the world's largest experiment without controls.

The Physiology of Lactation

The physiology of lactation involves the human mammary gland as well as the composition of human milk. The human mammary gland, the medical name for the breast, is the only organ not fully developed at birth. Congenital absence of the breast, *amastia,* is rare. The adult female gland consists of a branching system of excretory ducts embedded in connective tissue. Following the account of breast development and lactation in Lawrence and Lawrence (1999:Chapters 2 and 3), the mammary gland undergoes three phases of growth: in the uterus before birth, during childhood when the gland keeps pace with physical growth, and during the pubertal period.

In the fifth week of embryonic life, the paired breasts of the adult female develop from a line of glandular tissue in the fetus known as the milk lines. At six weeks, mammary glands begin to develop without hormonal stimulation. After 28 weeks of gestation, placental sex hormones enter fetal circulation. Near term, about 15 to 25 mammary ducts form the fetal mammary gland composed of glandular tissue, supporting connective tissue, and protective fatty tissue. Immediately after birth, the breasts of both male and female infants commonly swell and secrete a small amount of so-called witch's milk, because the same hormones that the placenta produces to prepare the mother's breasts for lactation also stimulate the infant's mammary glands. The secretions subside within three to four weeks and the mammary glands become inactive until shortly before the onset of puberty when hormones again stimulate growth.

When the female is 10 to 12 years old, the tree of ducts rapidly extends into a branching pattern. Alveolar buds form within a year or two of the onset of menses, and new buds sprout for several years, producing alveolar lobes. Female breasts enlarge to adult size at puberty, the left often larger than the right. Shape varies; it is typically dome or conic in adolescence, then more hemispheric, and finally pendulous in a woman who has borne children.

The skin of the breast includes the nipple, areola, and general skin. The nipple, located in the center of the areola, contains 15 to 25 milk ducts each of which open onto the nipple. Areola and nipple are darker than the rest of the breast, perhaps a visual signal to newborns so that they will close their mouth on the areola, not the nipple alone, to obtain milk.

Lactation is the physiological completion of the reproductive cycle. Without any active intervention by the mother, the breast is prepared for full lactation from 16 weeks gestation. Till the birth, the breast is kept inactive by a balance of inhibiting hormones that suppress target cell response.

At birth, a complex sequence of events governed by hormonal action prepares the breast for lactation. Between 40 to 72 hours after birth, a woman experiences milk coming in as a feeling of fullness. If she had earlier borne a child, she senses this more quickly than does the woman at her first birth. The volume of milk increases over time for the first two weeks, starting at less than 100 ml/day and rising to about 600 ml/day at 96 hours. Lactose, sodium chloride, and protein rise promptly and stabilize at 24 hours.

The lactating glands adjust milk supply to demand. Reduction in the sucking stimulus produces a reduction in the hormone prolactin and milk synthesis. Variation in milk secretion is reflected rapidly in anatomic change in the mammary gland. In the absence of stimulation, mammary tissue regresses the first week after birth. When a suckling infant signals its needs, the breast responds.

Unless frequent suckling or use of a breast pump empties the lactating breast, the glands become much distended and milk production gradually ceases. The absence of suckling initiates the neuron-hormonal reflex for the maintenance of prolactin secretion, and the ensuing engorgement of the breast causes diminished flow by compressing the blood vessels. Though the process of regression has been studied carefully in cows and other bovines, little study has been done in humans.

Numerous accounts in the medical literature indicate that breastfeeding can occur without pregnancy (Lawrence and Lawrence 1999:633). A woman who never gave birth can be induced to lactate, as can a woman who has given birth but did not breastfeed. A woman whose child is weaned can be induced to relactate. Historically, the motivation was to nourish an infant whose mother died or was unable to nurse. So-called induced lactation has been used in times of disaster to provide safe nutrition for weaned motherless infants. Currently, interest in induced lactation has been observed on the part of women who plan to adopt a child and hope to nurture it at the breast.

The process of induced lactation should begin several months before the adopted child is to arrive. Useful exercises include nipple stroking, massaging the breast, and rolling the nipple between thumb and finger or using a hand pump or other pumping devices (Lawrence and Lawrence 1999:641). Sometimes this process can produce a secretion if it be carried out daily on a uniform schedule.

When lactation is induced as an infant survival tactic, the infant is put to the adoptive mother's breast and allowed to suckle. In some cultures, the infant also may be given prechewed food, gruel, or animal milk. Provision for additional nourishment during the process of establishing milk secretion is important. The onset of lactation may vary from one to six weeks, averaging about four weeks after the initiation of stimulation. The difference in the techniques of sucking (as on a straw) and suckling (which involves moving the lips) may confuse some infants. To be most effective, a pharmacologic regimen to stimulate milk production should begin after the breast tissue has responded to mechanical stimulation.

The Composition of Human Milk

Scientists know much less about the nature of human milk than one might expect because the study of human lactation is so recent. Owing to its economic importance, the milk of cows, goats, and sheep was studied extensively during the twentieth century. By contrast, most of the research on human milk appeared only after 1970 (Lawrence 1994:91).

Anthropologists rarely gathered detailed data on breastfeeding, which was and remains very difficult to study in the shrinking number of populations that exercise no deliberate control over their fertility (Panter-Brick 1992:137). Volume and composition are hard to compare owing to differing procedures of weighing and testing, inconsistent extraction techniques, and variation in the sampling time between feeds (Jelliffe and Jelliffe 1978). Moreover, as studies rarely separate full and partial breastfeeding, averages tend to hide more than they reveal (Rodrigues and Diaz 1993:414). Retrospective surveys of mothers who have nursed their infants cost little to conduct but unfortunately tend to yield unreliable data (Haaga 1988:307), and interview data reveal a low concordance between timed data and the mother's memory of feeds (Vitzthum 1997:247). Direct observation of breastfeeding thus requires a huge investment in time. It is not surprising that few studies report such data (Ellison 1995:316). However, recent advances in technology have allowed the collection of much data about human milk.

Developed through the process of natural selection, human milk evolved to meet the singular needs of human infants. For example, the infant's need for lactose (milk sugar) is extraordinary, for its brain can grow only if it receives large amounts. At birth, the infant is the most immature and dependent of all mammals except for marsupials such as kangaroos. Unlike the brains of most other mammals, the human brain at birth is relatively small, only about one-quarter of full adult size.

The composition of human milk helps to explain both the duration and frequency of breast-feeding, both of which depend physiologically on early suckling to trigger projection and ejection of milk through processes regulated by hormones that have been described only in the past few decades (Quandt 1995:128). A hominid trait that evolved earlier was a milk content suited for infants who can nurse on demand. Infant chimpanzees, whose mother's milk is like that of the early and later hominids, also nurse at will for at least four years (Small 1998:185).

Compared with the milk of other mammals, the so-called mature milk of all primates, which appears about three weeks after birth, is dilute, very low in fat and protein but high in lactose, all of which affect frequency of suckling. Species that nurse less often have richer milk. A mother rabbit, for example, returns only once a day to the concealed spot where she has parked her offspring. By contrast, human milk is typical of a species that suckles its young almost continuously (Micozzi 1995:357).

Over time natural selection favored mothers who devised ways to keep their infants with them while they walked long distances in search of food like nuts and berries and small animals. Clever hominid females invented slings that enabled them to carry their young while they simultaneously used both hands to collect food.

The answers to some questions about human milk remain elusive, according to Lawrence and Lawrence (1999:Ch. 4). A question as simple as the volume of milk consumed at a feeding must deal adequately with several issues. The methodology must be accurate, reproducible, noninvasive, relatively easy to use at home, night or day, and must not interrupt the suckling. Milk composition constantly changes. The fat content increases toward the end of each feeding and rises from early morning to midday, and earlier milk differs from later milk in the same feeding. Composition varies with stage of lactation, time of day, sampling time, and maternal nutrition. Pumped samples vary from those obtained by suckling and the content varies among various methods of pumping. Many early interpretations of milk content were in error because they were based on pooled samples from multiple donors at different times and stages of lactations.

The mother's diet is a major concern in studies of variation in milk content. Should her diet be inadequate, many of the nutrients in the milk come from her body rather than from her diet. The milk of a malnourished mother has about the same proportions of protein, fat, and carbohydrate as that of a well-nourished one but the malnourished woman produces less milk. Poor diet affects vitamins in the milk that are water soluble such as ascorbic acid and thiamine but even if the mother's diet is imperfect, the benefits of human milk normally outweigh the drawbacks.

The identifiable stages of human milk are those of colostrum, transitional milk, and mature milk. The first week after birth, mammary secretion consists of a yellowish, thick fluid, colostrum, which is rich in antibodies that may protect against the bacteria and viruses present in the birth canal. Such pathogens are also available all too easily from contacts with other humans. The high protein and low fat content of colostrum are consonant with infant needs at birth. Historically, not all societies recognized the value of colostrum and some social customs called for feeding other concoctions to the infant for several days (Fildes 1988:25).

The content of the transitional milk, which appears seven to ten days after birth, gradually changes. The protein and immunoglobulin content decrease while the lactose, fat, and caloric content rise. The so-called mature milk appears when the infant is about two or three weeks old. Because the chief content of almost all mammal milk is water, a lactating woman needs to drink much more of it. If maternal water intake is restricted during lactation, the loss of water through urine declines before water for lactation diminishes in quantity. Even in a hot climate the infant's entire water requirement can be provided by human milk.

The Discovery of Natural Fertility

In the memory of people who are still living, demography professors taught students that Malthus got it right: population numbers always tend to outstrip the food supply. Disasters like fire, flood, and famine held human numbers in check. The only way humans could control population size was total abstinence from sexual relations.

The discovery of a so-called natural way to control fertility was relatively late in coming. Not until the 1960s and 1970s did the idea begin to get around that frequent and prolonged suckling brought ovulation to a halt. The interval of amenorrhea (absence of menstrual periods) indicates the absence of ovulation, thus the inability to conceive a child. Amenorrhea lasts about two months or a little less in women who do not breastfeed (Leridon 1977).

Premodern populations knew that breastfeeding affected infant and child mortality (Wood 1994:33), but their consciousness of the effect of suckling on amenorrhea is not certain. Fildes (1986:12) thinks that at least some of the ancients knew that lactation prevented conception. By contrast, some contemporary peoples living south of the Sahara were said to be unaware of the effects of lactation on fertility despite common knowledge that sickness and death often followed abrupt weaning (van de Walle and van de Walle 1993:69, 547). Whatever the state of popular belief about lactation as a contraceptive, it was not long ago that Western medical science defined the claim that it prevented pregnancy as an old wives' tale (Vitzthum 1997:244). Only 30 years ago, for example, physician Thomas McKeown (1976:73), who was unaware of the effect of frequent and prolonged lactation on ovulation, claimed that infanticide was common until the late 1800s. The scheduled pattern of nursing that follows from biomedical models of infant rearing (a pattern not often found in most populations) helps to explain this belief. The medical model (which was devised in the absence of detailed knowledge about the characteristics of human milk) recommends spacing feeds two to five hours apart, nursing for five to twenty minutes at each feed. As this mode of breastfeeding minimally suppressed ovarian function, it led biomedical health practitioners to doubt until recently that there was any relationship between lactation and fecundity (Vitzthum 1994:316).

Demographers were also slow to see the significance of child spacing patterns in the premodern era, and economists were slower still (Page and Lesthaeghe 1981:ix). As recently as the 1950s, population scientists apparently were unaware of the effects of lactation on amenorrhea and infecundity (Hobcraft 1994:413). Frank Lorimer's (1954) influential UNESCO volume on culture and human fertility did not discuss any effects of lactation, nor did Kingsley Davis and Judith Blake (1956) make any mention of it in their landmark paper that claimed to list all of the intermediate variables that determine fertility (Ellison 1995:305).

As late as the 1980s the study of paleodemography continued to be based on the Malthusian idea that prehistoric populations were characterized by both high fertility and high mortality. Where natural checks on fertility were too low, scholars generally believed that cultural practices such as infanticide and abortion controlled population levels. These controls were considered to be especially important among hunting and gathering populations because this mode of subsistence and the carrying capacity of the environment dictated low population numbers lest an increasing number of children threaten the food supply (Bentley 1996:26).

Not until the 1950s did French demographer Louis Henry (1953) define natural fertility as the absence of deliberate control, that is, when a couple's behavior is neither bound to the number of children born nor modified when this number reaches the maximum the couple wants (Menken 1977:3). A few years later, Gioiosa (1955) proposed that a major function of human lactation beyond its nutritional and immunological benefits might be its role as a natural birth spacer, and Louis Henry (1961) boldly suggested that lactation might be the primary determinant of natural fertility (Ellison 1995:338).

In the 1970s, detailed ethnodemographic data on foragers in the Kalahari desert revealed much lower mortality and fertility than had been previously supposed (Lee and DeVore 1976), a lifetime average of five births (Howell 1979:291). A little later an international conference sponsored by the World Health Organization, the Rockefeller Foundation, and Family Health International announced that breast-feeding was a safe and effective contraceptive (Ellison 1995:305).

However, it was not clear until the 1990s why the effectiveness of breastfeeding in suppressing fertility so varied among both individuals and societies. It is now known that the suppression of ovulation depends on the strength of the sucking stimulus and its impact on secretion of the hormones prolactin and gonadotrophin (McNeilley 1993).

When the time given over to suckling diminishes beyond a certain point, ovulation will occur even though the mother has continued to breastfeed the infant. An Edinburgh study reported, for example, that every one of the mothers who ovulated while they were breastfeeding had introduced two or more supplementary feeds each day, which enabled them to reduce suckling to fewer than six periods a day. The amount of time spent in suckling, reduced by 60 minutes, permitted the resumption of ovulation (Lawrence and Lawrence 1999:658).

Demographers who study the fertility patterns of the past now agree that natural fertility was almost universal before the demographic transition that began in Western Europe in the late 1700s (Wood 1990:213; Xie 1991). Wood (1994:9) holds that this conclusion runs counter to a widespread conviction among ethnographers that social customs control fertility, for example, customs concerning infanticide or the postpartum restriction on sexual intercourse in societies that permitted polygyny. Barring women who are lactating from engaging in sexual intercourse was one way to keep women in their place (Caldwell and Caldwell 1981:193). Belief in the cultural control of fertility may prove to be especially resistant to change among feminists. Conkey and Gero (1997:417) have claimed that the idea that sex and gender are social constructions rooted neither in biology nor in procreation has been integral to feminist thought since the early 1970s.

Why the suppression of fertility caused by breastfeeding varied not only by individual but also by culture is likewise more clear. It is now thought that the high variation in total fertility rates in natural fertility populations is due to varied intensity and duration of breastfeeding and to age of marriage (Wood 1990:233). Frequency and strength of the sucking stimulus is critical (see references in Zohoori and Popkin 1996:167). Longitudinal studies now confirm that decreases in either the frequency or the duration of suckling spur the resumption of ovarian activity (McNeilly 1993:394).

Thus did we humans come to embody mechanisms that have enabled us to produce infants who are twice as likely as those of our primate cousins to live long enough to produce offspring. Frequent and prolonged suckling became customary among foragers because it prevented a new birth until the older child could walk the long distances required in the daily search for food. Among populations who depended on the hoe or plow or upon herding large animals to obtain their food, the pattern was much the same because the supplementary foods that were available were generally contaminated. Adults often sickened on such foods. Small children were likely not only to sicken but also die from the dehydration induced by diarrhea. Thus, before the discovery of the germ theory of disease and the invention of techniques of sterilization, the prolonged and frequent suckling of human milk displaced dangerous supplements of spoiled food, and maximized a child's chances of survival.

Physiological and Social Benefits and Costs of Breastfeeding

Research on human milk, conducted by scholars in the biological and physical sciences, has focused on the physiology of lactation. Human milk is the complex result of the long evolution of a product that met the specific needs of the human infant far better than any formula devised in a laboratory. The physiological benefits of breastfeeding to mother and infant are high and the costs are modest for both. The social benefits and costs are another story. For infants, benefits are high (and well documented) and costs are nil while the mother's social benefits are modest but her social costs are very high owing to women's exclusion from the activities that bring high prestige.

Benefits and Costs for Infant

Because the composition of human breast milk results from a long evolutionary process that favored the qualities that contributed the most to infant survival, it is no surprise that breast milk provides the ideal nutrients for human growth during the first year of life. The infant's ability to digest and absorb human milk is highly efficient compared with that for cow's milk from which only a small fraction of some nutrients is absorbed.

An important benefit of breastfeeding for the infant is that it not only minimizes infection by decreasing or eliminating consumption of pathogenic bacteria and viruses that may contaminate other food but also provides the antibodies that the mother has developed against diseases common to the infant's environment. A newborn lacks enough innate defenses to protect against the environmental contamination it encounters after it has benefited from the sterile uterine environment. Its gastro-intestinal tract, upper and lower respiratory systems, and urinary tract are especially vulnerable to pathogens.

Human milk also includes related defense mechanisms of which most people are unaware, according to Nesse and Williams (1994:29ff) whose account I follow. The bacteria that enjoy feasting on human bodies strongly prefer large amounts of iron, a crucial and scarce resource for them. Their human hosts have evolved a wide variety of mechanisms to keep bacteria from getting the iron they need. One is the evolution of molecules that bind iron so that it does not circulate freely in the blood. Too much iron in the blood can make for serious infections. The protein in human milk is 20 percent lactoferrin, a molecule designed to bind iron; cow's milk has only about two percent of it. Breast-fed babies consequently have fewer infections than those fed from bottles.

Breast-fed infants also have a much lower incidence of acute infection of the inner ear than those fed by bottle, in part because sucking and suckling differ mechanically. When an infant sucks on a rubber nipple, the action fails to close the Eustachian tube in its middle ear. If the infant later regurgitates any of its meal, the contents of the stomach may enter the Eustachian tube and fester there, especially since the bottle-fed infant lacks the antibodies that would have been available in its mother's milk (see Lawrence and Lawrence 1999:236, 242).

Breast milk also protects the infant against the development of common allergies such as eczema and asthma. The introduction to the infant diet and even to the mother's diet of proteins other than those in breast milk can lead to allergies. Even exclusive breastfeeding will not protect children with a strong family history of allergy unless the mother excludes from her diet common allergens like cow's milk, eggs, peanuts, and wheat.

The physiological costs of breastfeeding, save for a few infections that are readily treatable, are minimal for the infant. Acute infectious diseases in the mother are usually treatable, and by the time someone diagnoses maternal illness, the infant usually has already been exposed to it. The best management generally is to continue breastfeeding so that the infant receives the mother's antibodies.

However, a few specific infections can overwhelm the protective mechanisms of breast milk. The most prominent one currently is the human immunodeficiency virus (HIV) and the acquired immunodeficiency syndrome (AIDS). Scholars currently advise the curtailment of breastfeeding should the mother test positively for either disease.

The social benefits of breastfeeding are harder to measure than the physiological ones. For example, an infant has been diagnosed and hospitalized for a specific ailment or it has not. By contrast, the measurement of qualities such as degree of social adjustment tends to be slippery. Nonetheless, it seems likely that the social benefits for the infant are great though it would be difficult to demonstrate that holding all else equal breastfeeding provides more social benefits than does bottle feeding. Advice books for mothers generally reassure their readers that a mother can be warm, loving, and nurturing even if she is unable to breastfeed. However, because the mother of a bottle-fed infant may choose to delegate the task, she may have less control over the quality of nurturing that the infant receives.

The social costs of breastfeeding to the infant are nil.

Benefits and Costs for Mother

The physiological benefits of breastfeeding to the mother are substantial. In the mid-twentieth century, a number of medical books reported that women who breast-fed their infants returned to a prepregnancy state more rapidly than women who did not and also had a lower incidence of obesity later in life.

Relatively late in the twentieth century, researchers recognized another benefit of great importance for both mother and infant. Study of female hormonal effects on natural fertility demonstrated that ovulation resumed in the absence of lactation. The huge decrease in the frequency and duration of breastfeeding today among Western women thus has resulted in the flooding of their bodies with a variety of hormones during a much larger proportion of the reproductive period than occurred when the ancient mode of breastfeeding prevailed. Modern women experience an average of 450 menstrual cycles over a lifetime vs. 50 cycles for women who breastfeed in the ancient mode (see citations in Crews and Gerber 1994:159; Stuart-Macadam 1998:57).

The net effect of modern patterns of lactation thus is to increase the exposure of reproductive tissues to estrogenic hormones which, in turn, increases the proliferation of cells (Maynard Smith et al. 1999:270). For example, the turnover rates of duct cells in the breast are up to 20 times higher between menarche and first birth than after the first full-term pregnancy. Cells that divide often are more likely to develop clinical malignancy. Women in affluent societies thus carry a risk of malignancy that is from 10 to 100 fold greater than that experienced by women foragers.

Significantly, the rates of diseases linked to chronic hormone exposure are rising for both sexes: endometrial, colon, breast, and prostate cancer as well as coronary heart disease (Micozzi 1995; Whitten 1999:211). The incidence of cancers likely reflects the transformation of human biology that has accompanied the profound ecological changes of modernization.

Rather than wait for a magic bullet, we may have to work, or at least exercise, to reduce the rate of reproductive cancers (Ellison 1999:201). Nesse and Williams (1994:181) suggest that with ever more detailed knowledge of the physiological effects of natural and artificial hormones, we should be increasingly able to devise artificial ways of mimicking the beneficial effects of forager life histories, and that this may not be as utopian a possibility as it might seem. Interventional endocrinology, including menarche delay, early pseudopregnancy, and estrogen-lowering oral contraception could perhaps recreate an ancestral hormonal milieu (Maynard Smith et al. 1999:270).

Nonetheless, abundant calories and fats currently increase the exposure to gonadal steroids by lowering the age of puberty (Worthman 1999b). Privileged populations become developmental outliers, pushing the envelope of the human maturation rate. Adult behavior does not suffice to explain the rising global prevalence of chronic conditions like cancer, hypertension, diabetes, and obesity (Worthman 1999a:91).

The physiological costs of breastfeeding to the mother involve breast infections that modern medicine can usually cure but are most common in women who are breastfeeding (Komaroff 1999:1053–4). Two types occur: mastitis and abscesses. Mastitis is an inflammation of the breast tissue usually due to a blocked milk duct in which bacteria multiply. The bacteria normally live on the skin or in the mouth of the nursing infant and are transferred to the breast during nursing. A breast abscess, an uncommon bacterial infection that produces a pus-filled sac in the soft tissues beneath the skin or in a milk duct, can occur when mastitis is not properly treated or during the early weeks of breastfeeding when cracked nipples may make it easier for bacteria to infect the breast.

The social benefits to the mother are more difficult to assess. Lawrence and Lawrence (1999:219) say that breastfeeding empowers a woman to do something special for her infant. They believe that holding the infant to her breast to provide total nutrition and nurturing results in an even more profound psychological experience than carrying the fetus in the uterus. It is difficult to argue with the proposition that many women take profound satisfaction in their ability to nourish their infant.

The social costs of breastfeeding are another matter. It is interesting that in discussions of the costs of breastfeeding neither the manuals that give advice on child care nor economic studies of the cost of breastfeeding have much to say about the opportunity cost of the mother's time. The primary cost stems from the content of human milk: high in lactose, low in protein and fat. An infant hungers often because it digests sugars rapidly. That is why the average time between feeds was about 15 minutes in the ancient mode of lactation. The need to feed an infant often precludes the mother's engaging in a variety of other activities. A forager infant could get enough to eat only if its mother remained nearby until the child could walk long distances. The danger of eating contaminated food made the same prolonged period of suckling optimal for infant health until the invention of ways to ensure the safety of drinking water and food.

However, the social costs of lactation clearly have differed by time and place because women's work has varied with the ecology and technology of food production. The social costs to mothers were probably lowest among foragers and highest in plow cultures. The absence of women in politically powerful positions enabled elite men to devise social systems that constrained wives by law and custom, systems that were shored up by the ideological justifications formulated by the more powerful in all human groups to explain and justify the distribution of goods to the less powerful. The next chapter considers variation in the social constraints of lactation in more detail.

Chapter Five

Subsistence Modes and Infant Diet

THE IDEA THAT HUMAN VALUES AND CUSTOMS are a purely social construction is a roadmap to a dead end. Causal analysis must be based on variables rooted in the real world (e.g., soil fertility, climate, technology, terrain) that offer differentiating average conditions in which people employ routines adapted to local conditions and the resources that make the routines practical (Rytina 2000:2824). An example is Gerhard Lenski's (1970; 2005) ecological-evolutionary approach to human stratification. Jared Diamond (1997; 2002), an apparently magisterial social scientist, demonstrated how the interplay of ecology and technology enabled Northwest Europeans to dominate the world. In this chapter I compare infant diet in foraging, hoe, herding, and plow societies in order to show how ecology and technology have affected beliefs and behaviors concerning the feeding of human offspring.

In hoe and herding societies, infant diet consisted of human milk as it had in forager groups, with one exception. In the event of maternal disability or death, a variety of soft foods and animal milk was available, though such foods were risky because they spoiled so easily. The emergence of very rich hoe and herding societies and of plow societies led to a second exception. The size of the surplus enabled elite couples to hire a so-called wet nurse to suckle their own infant. Because a human female rarely has enough milk to feed two babies, the hiring of a wet nurse sharply reduced the life chances of a subset of unlucky infants who had been born to slave or poor peasant women.

The constraints on human diet are a consequence of the interplay of ecology, technology, and human organization. Not long ago, most social scientists followed Malthus in believing that human inventions led to an increase in the food supply that in turn increased the rate of population growth. According to this view, the innovations in subsistence production that began about 10,000 years ago stimulated the ensuing growth of human populations. Then Danish economist Ester Boserup (1965) turned Malthus on his head: It was the increase in population size and subsequent need to feed more people that spurred inventions, not the other way around. Hungry people think of new ways to produce more food (Cohen 1984:1, but see Stone and Downum 1999).

But there was a cost. Digging stick, hoe, and plow can make land more productive but only with greater input of human labor. People do not turn the soil, fodder animals, or collect manure unless they must (Netting 1993:103). The technologies historically hailed as a liberating force were better seen as a holding action (Cohen 1977:285).

Because the sensory factors that evolved during hominoid evolution influenced the food choices of both ape and human, I first discuss the diet our ancestors consumed for millions of years before hunger compelled them to domesticate plants and animals. I then show how ecology and technology affected human diet in societies based on hoe, herding, and the plow technology in order to convey the nature of the problems that infant diet posed for our ancestors.

The Primate Fruit Diet

The basis of primate food sensibilities was a diet based primarily on fruit. The discussion below follows Nesse and Williams

(1994) and Whitten (1999:210–43). Fruits are unique plant products in that they evolved as sugary lures that gave seeds a free ride in an animal gut to a distant germination site. Given fruits survived the selection process because they could attract the animals that were most adapted to disperse the seeds at the best time and place. Seeds are often especially poisonous because their destruction at the wrong time thwarts the plant's reproductive strategy. Eating the fruit before the seeds are ready wastes an entire investment, thus many plants make potent poisons to discourage consumption of immature fruits (Nesse and Williams 1994:80). All fruits signal appropriate animal vectors that the flesh is sweet, soft, and succulent when the seeds are ready for a trip in a warm and moist gut to a good site for deposit and germination of that particular type of seed.

Ripening is heralded by bright colors that make fruit stand out from leaves while the bitter and astringent chemicals like tannins that are highly concentrated in unripe fruit decline. To make subtle judgments about ripeness, nutrient content, and plant defenses (which humans generally perceive as bitter), fruit eaters developed a nuanced sense of color, texture, and taste. Primates regained the color vision that had been lost in the nocturnal origins of mammals (though it remained widely distributed among fish, reptiles and birds), and became most sensitive to those parts of the color spectrum that signal the changes in ripening fruit: yellow-orange, yellow, and blue-green. As they ripen, primate-dispersed fruits take on yellow-orange hues while bird-dispersed fruits take on red, blue, white, and purple colors.

Global colonization and adaptation to local ecosystems resulted in a broader array of diets in human populations, but we probably have the same perceptual bases for food choice as did our ancestors. Though fruit is no longer the main staple in human diet, we still prefer food with a nutrient and chemical content much like that of the foods relished by apes. Appearance and taste that reflect ancient biochemical defenses mediate our preferences, for the relatively short history of domestication of plants makes it unlikely that our physiological ability to process food chemicals has diverged much from that of our ancestors. Ancestral diets, like our own, carried both costs and benefits. All human diets include toxins. This dictum is one of the less welcome conclusions that arise from an evolutionary view of medicine (Nesse and Williams, 1994:86).

Hunter-gatherers added seeds, roots, and herbaceous tubers that they could more easily collect and store than the fruits of tropical hardwoods. Overall, forager foods were denser in energy than were ape foods owing to their higher fat and lower fiber content (see references in Whitten 1999). As measured by general levels of health, humans are more adapted to a forager diet than to those that replaced it as human populations spread over the globe. An example is scurvy, marked by swollen gums, livid spots on the skin, and prostration. The disease arose among peoples who, by moving north, lost easy access to fresh fruit. It often afflicted British sailors on long voyages. The adding of lime juice to their diet cured them and led to their being called "Limeys." Fruits that are rich in vitamin C were so important in primate diet for so long that the biochemical machinery to make the vitamin degenerated in all humans and even in some apes (Nesse and Williams 1994:130).

The subsistence technologies adopted by the societies that replaced forager groups increased food production but incurred costs that directly or indirectly affected infant diet. The costs included higher levels of social inequality, more frequent warfare, and substantial declines in human health. The temporal ordering of herding and hoe cultures has not been established, but plow cultures worldwide appeared later than those based on herding or hoe, and the grain diet that prevailed in the plow kingdoms and empires of Eurasia posed especially serious problems for human health.

Foragers

Forager (hunter-gatherer) groups exhibited a level of social equality as high as any ever known among humans (Martin and Voorhies 1975; Sanday 1971; Blumberg 1984; Chafetz

1984). In the 1970s and early 1980s scholars aware of feminist issues debated whether or not such groups were truly or only relatively equalitarian. Feminists tried to document the absence of sex inequality in order to prove that biology did not determine women's secondary status. Marxists hoped to show that equality prevailed in the absence of private property (Huber 1999:69).

In retrospect, it seems likely that some level of social inequality is unavoidable in all societies because nature has endowed all humans except identical twins with mental and physical abilities that differentially advantage or challenge them in the competition for material resources and social esteem. However, sexual inequality likely was low among foragers. Women's contribution to subsistence was high, people were few, land was plentiful, and crowding minimal (one person to a square mile). Warfare was rare; groups could readily avoid one another in the food search (Johnson and Earle 1987).

As women's gathering yielded more calories on average than did men's hunting, the incentives for group control of sexuality were low. Casual sex and frequent divorce were common (Collins et al. 1993:199). There was no steady surplus of food because storage was impossible. Typically, each woman nursed only her own infant, for few women have enough milk for more than one child. A woman usually carried her youngest child in a sling while she collected food. As it was hard to feed and carry two infants, foragers tended to believe that twins brought bad luck. The mother might have to kill one or both (depending on group norms), usually by exposure. In lean times, parents might have to kill one of their children when they had too many mouths to feed.

Humans give up foraging as a way of life when they can no longer find solutions to the problem of local resource failure. The hunting and gathering way of life supports fewer than one person per square mile (Konner 1982:9). Searching for new ways to assure their food supply, erstwhile foragers turned to a semisedentary mode of life based on the use of digging stick or hoe in areas of abundant rainfall. Where rainfall was too scant or the terrain too rough to permit growing crops, they turned to the herding of sheep, cattle, or goats. Though these two modes differ considerably, the level of technology that underlies them is much the same. Our ancestors domesticated animals at about the same time as plants.

Hoe Societies

The use of digging stick and metal-tipped hoe produced more resources than did foraging, but these tools require more labor input. To grow crops in tropical forest or grassland savanna, men must clear the land of wild vegetation before planting (Friedl 1975:59ff). After a few years it must lie fallow for as long as ten years, and then be cleared again to grow sweet potato, taro, yam, and banana in tropical areas like the Pacific Islands and parts of West Africa or tapioca and cassava in tropical South America. East Africa and parts of North and South America produce cereal crops like the millets and maize; rice is grown in parts of south Asia. Domesticated animals like cattle or pigs become prestige objects in exchange as well as a source of meat and sometimes milk.

Thus, in hoe cultures, which are characterized by relatively low population density and shifting tillage, women do most of the work using hand tools. Polygyny, a form of marriage that permits a man to marry more than one woman at a time, is one way to increase production. Custom holds that a man can become rich only if he has many wives. A man seeking a bride often must pay the so-called bride-price to compensate her father for the loss of her services.

Men monopolized three activities. One was the clearing of the land. Later, either sex could plant, harvest, and transport crops, for a woman can do this work while toting a nursling in a sling. Older children tended younger ones. Hoe cultures thus displayed the gender role diversity that became the basis for the relativist view of human belief and behavior promulgated by Boas and his students. Patterns of marriage and kinship tended to follow the division of labor, for the control of labor is crucial (Friedl 1975).

Men also monopolized war. In hoe cultures all adult males served as part-time warriors; women rarely served (Davie 1929:30–4; Wright 1942:84). Before the 1960s, anthropologists rarely studied war (Otterbein 1999:796), and the views of one of the few who did were widely accepted. Turney-High (1949) held that primitive war was more athletic contest than military exercise. By contrast, recent studies suggest that primitive war was an extremely bloody business in which men, women, and children suffered great harm (LeBlanc 1999). Collins et al. (1993) have shown how war spurs the emergence of sexual politics that result in the segregation of men's and women's activities, to be discussed in the next chapter.

The third male monopoly involved political participation. Women's near absence from politics paralleled their absence from war. An extensive search reported that women were political actors in only a few societies in Africa and North America (Hobhouse et al. 1930:176–215). I explain the connection of war and politics in Chapter 6.

It was the success of efforts to restrict resources that marked the beginnings of warfare (Johnson and Earle 1987:58). Biologists make no case for a pervasive aggressive instinct but rather see most aggressive behavior as a response to environmental crowding (Wilson 1996:84). Humans are obliged to solve the same ecological problems as other species in order to produce children who live long enough to reproduce (Ember and Ember 1992; Low, Clarke, and Lockridge 1992). Population pressure spurs the formation of local groups five to ten times larger than a typical family to act on issues of food storage and defense.

A chief could organize a region if he could establish control over warfare, large-scale technology, central storage, and external trade (Johnson and Earle 1987:245). In kin-based tribal groups, the structure of kinship serves as an organization of coercion that upholds the property system (Collins et al. 1993:199). The more often a society engaged in warfare, the more likely was social control to be vested in politico-military elites that excluded women (see Collins 1988:168–73). The effects of sexual politics came to a peak in herding and agrarian societies when a military aristocracy ruled a disarmed peasantry.

Herding Societies

Pastoral economies, which cover the technological range of societies based on the hoe and the wooden plow, appeared in areas where tillage was difficult owing to mountainous terrain, a short growing season, or low rainfall, as in Central Asia, Arabia, North Africa, and parts of Europe and of sub-Saharan Africa (Lenski and Lenski 1978:235). Owing to historical accident, herding societies uniquely influenced much of Europe, West Asia, Southeast Asia, North Africa, and both North and South America. The gender norms of ancient Hebrew herders and traders often became embedded in law and custom across the lands that had been strongly influenced by the political and military victories of both Christian and Muslim conquerors (Huber 1999).

Moving livestock to seasonal pastures to convert grass into human food requires a nomadic or seminomadic way of life. The use of spatial mobility as a survival strategy may lead to competition with agrarians over territory and disputes over water and stolen animals (Beck 1978:52). Meanwhile, the constant threat of conflict during migration stimulates the growth and consolidation of centralized political authority, especially because the open grasslands where most herders live pose few barriers to movement and political consolidation. A herding society may be as huge as the Asian empire of Ghenghis Khan, but the size of a herding community is typically only a little larger than that of a forager group because a small unit can more easily maintain a herd in areas where scanty rainfall limits the food supply.

Almost three thousand years ago Asian herders acquired a huge advantage over less mobile agrarians in the waves of conquest that ensued after they had learned to ride their horses. Herding groups repeatedly devastated Eurasian agrarian empires over a period of more than 2500 years (Lenski and Lenski 1978:237–318). Bubonic plague (the Black Death) had long festered in Asia but it became epidemic only when Mongol invaders brought it to previously unexposed communities in Europe who lived with large populations of flea-infested rats given to dining on the resources produced by the plow (Nesse and Williams 1994:64).

Scholars and travelers were long attracted to romantic stereotypes of fierce and independent nomads who defined all virtues as male. Anthropologists neglected the role of women in pastoral societies until after the 1970s. A careful study has yet to be made of the way that women and men influence decisions on resource allocation (Dyson-Hudson and Dyson-Hudson 1980). The study of sex inequality in herding societies is currently especially difficult because many of them also depend on the use of hoe or plow, tools that oppositely affect women's economic productivity, and the gathering of cross-cultural data on lactation is especially problematic in a mobile population that does not track chronological age (Wiley and Pike 1988). Most of the data on infant feeding among herders dates from the 1980s, and by then few herders could avoid at least minimal contact with plow and industrial peoples.

Valuable data on infant feeding among contemporary nomads are reported in Little and Leslie's (1999) study of nomad biobehavioral response to an uncertain environment among the Turkana, an East African ethnic group who resented the British because they made Turkana men build roads and forts when in fact among the Turkana it was the women who lifted and carried the heavy loads. The data are of great interest; quantified descriptions of the old-style are rare (R. Dyson-Hudson 1999:39).

Gray (1999:167) reports that breastfeeding in herding societies can be characterized by four practices. The ritual touching of the infant's lips with goat's or cow's milk that preceded the infant's being given the breast; on-demand breastfeeding lasting 18 to 24 months; introduction of some form of milk fat in the infant's first month; and the gradual introduction of animal milk during the child's first year (Gray 1999:167). A Turkana mother suckled her infant whenever it demanded the breast. The suckling events lasted less than 2.5 minutes and occurred at 10 to 15 minute intervals during the day. At night and during daytime naps, the nursling slept at its mother's nipple. Mothers said that they did not usually waken when their infants nursed. Only mothers of children aged 19 months or older reported maternal absences of more than 30 minutes to an hour.

Plow Societies

If rainfall and terrain permitted, a more complex technology involved use of the plow, which first appeared in West Asia about 5,000 years ago. Techniques to smelt iron invented about 2000 years later provided the plow with an iron blade. As iron is a common metal, plowshares proliferated and food production skyrocketed.

Large stores of food make a tempting target and plenty of iron was available in parts of West Asia to beat into both plowshares and swords, hence warfare became widespread. It has remained so ever since, which illustrates a general rule of human organization: The larger the food supply, the greater the temptation to control production and distribution (Lenski 1971). Elites, especially when they have access to weapons, speedily yield to temptation in the absence of a system of legitimated impulse control.

It was their perception of this principle that led the authors of the U.S. Constitution to institute a system of checks and balances to squelch impulsive behavior on the part of various factions that, then as now, wanted more than their fair share of resources. Such controls are nigh impossible in nonliterate societies. It is very difficult to introduce democratic institutions in areas in which many persons cannot read.

From its West Asian beginnings, plow technology spread to Europe, East Asia, and North Africa wherever temperature and rainfall permitted the cultivation of grain crops. In sub-Saharan Africa, the plow was rare because oxen, the best draft animals, can thrive neither in the humid zones of Central Africa nor in the West African coastal zones owing to the presence of the tse-tse fly, whose behavior during its complex life cycle enables it to severely weaken or kill both cattle and humans (Shipton 1994:357).

With higher population density and settled agriculture, men did most of the heavy work. Women became economic liabilities, in need of a dowry as a basis of support (Boserup 1970:35). The less food they produce, the more they are valued only as mothers, which results in different strategies of inheritance in tropical Africa and Eurasia owing to the effect of the plow on the respective value of land and level of women's economic productivity (Goody 1976:97). In African hoe cultures, for example, economic differences among families are minor, land is plentiful, and there is almost no pressure to provide an heir to an estate (Goody and Tambiah 1973:22). A daughter's marriage little affects her economic position because women, married or not, grow crops or do craft work. A daughter needs no endowment to maintain her livelihood.

The most obvious effect of the plow was a vast increase in the Eurasian food supply because continuous cultivation became possible for the first time, reducing the number of weeds and turning the soil deeply enough to restore fertility (Huber 1999). The invention of the plow spurred the domestication of draft animals (Lenski 1970). Confining the creatures in stalls to prevent their wandering off encouraged the collection of manure to fertilize the fields. Scattering manure on the fields magnificently affected food production. The invention of writing soon followed after, the better to keep track of a surplus large enough to be stored. Early on, Moses became famous as a bureaucrat, for he could keep track of the pharaoh's granaries in the fertile valley of the Nile.

Eurasian stratification patterns assumed the pyramidal form common to feudalism: a politico-economic elite at the top followed by a slim layer of merchants, artisans, and craft workers of lesser rank; and at the bottom, a multitude of peasants, serfs, or slaves. Use of the plow devastated the lives of ordinary people. A food surplus in the countryside coupled with the availability of iron weapons tempted elites to extract as much as possible from impoverished peasants (Goody 1976). The flatter and richer the land and the more food it could produce, the worse off were the men and women who did the work, probably much worse off than their forager ancestors (Lenski 1970).

The plow depressed women's status more than it did men's. One reason was that men generally monopolized its use. The plow, which required the management of heavy draft animals in larger fields further from home, was incompatible with the requirements of suckling an infant. Women's food production plummeted. With oxen, a man could plow in a day an area far larger than a woman could till by hoe (Childe 1951:100).

The plow's most significant effect on women's status resulted from the great rise in economic productivity and occupational specialization it permitted. Land became the chief form of wealth because a family could till a given piece in perpetuity. Individual land ownership gave rise to laws and customs that reflected elite men's monopoly not only on warfare but also on related political and economic institutions.

Rule and custom ensured that no one could subdivide land into segments too small to support a family. A holding of given size under a given technology can support only a limited number of persons. The scarcer land became and the more intensively it was used, the greater was the tendency to retain it in the nuclear family, the basic unit of human production and reproduction (Goody 1976:97).

Monogamy prevailed. Where Roman Catholicism was dominant, canon law decreed that divorce be difficult or impossible lest too many heirs legally claim a given property, a topic I soon discuss. In all plow societies, the concern with women's sexual purity became acute, for women were the transmitters of male property. The larger a woman's endowment, the more her sexual behavior was controlled. Monogamy constrained men less as their out-of-wedlock children could not inherit property. The children of the concubines and mistresses of wealthy European or Asian men had few if any inheritance rights.

Several customs attest the steep decline in women's status in Eurasian and North African agrarian societies (Huber and Spitze 1983:18–20). The lower the value of a woman's labor, the less that maiming her body affects the production of foodstuffs. Women are in a bad fix when ecology and technology permit the emergence of an ideology that defines a woman primarily as a mother.

An elite husband in Western Europe could lock a chastity belt around his wife's private parts and carry away the key were he to be away for a period of time on a crusade or other military expedition. The device prevented her having sexual intercourse. I have found no description as to how she kept herself clean while locked into the device.

In North African regions of plow use like Egypt, Yemen, Ethiopia, Somalia, the Sudan, and parts of Muslim West Africa, the practice of clitoridectomy was common (El Saadawi 1982:33; Hosken 1979). Older women performed the operation on prepubertal girls. The procedure was designed to prevent sexual pleasure by the cutting away of the clitoral prepuce and tip, the entire clitoris, or the clitoris along with the labia minora, and part of the labia majora, scraping the two sides raw and then sewing them together except for a tiny opening to let urine or (later) menstrual blood drain, all of this without the use of any drugs that might reduce the pain, or sanitary measures that would reduce the chances of serious infection. Consequences included chronic urinary infection and difficulties in childbirth and coitus. The custom still exists in parts of North Africa and among North African migrants elsewhere, including the United States. *The Economist* recently reported that it affects 130,000,000 women across the world.

In the subcontinent of India, the elite Hindu custom of suttee involved burning the widow alive on her husband's funeral pyre. The orthodox rationalization held that she had caused her husband to die before she did because of her sins in a previous life (Stein 1978:255). Some widows willingly climbed onto the pyre. Others did not. If a widow screamed and cried, her husband's male relatives simply tied her down. The wife's death gave the control of the estate to the husband's brothers.

In China, foot-binding was widespread in the wheat-growing areas of the north (Levy 1966). Legend says the custom began when an emperor admired a dancer's feet; the finished product resembled somewhat the leg and foot of a ballet dancer. The degree of maiming depended on the amount of work a woman was expected to do. The bindings generally were applied when the little girl was about three years old. The exceedingly painful process, completed soon after puberty, is a little like the work an orthodontist does to fit the teeth into the jaw, but the orthodontist tries hard not to hurt you lest you complain to your parents who are footing the bill (Huber and Spitze 1983). Successive tightening left the foot inches shorter than otherwise, and made normal walking nearly impossible. The custom was less common in the south where women worked in the rice paddies. Constant wading in filthy water could lead to serious infection.

A recent study concluded that the customs that began by restricting elite women's sexual freedom resulted in a socially competitive upward flow of maimed women paralleled by the downward flow of self-enforcing customs that were maintained by sex-linked needs on the marriage market. Women needed resources; men wanted certain knowledge of paternity (Mackie 1996).

An unanswered question is why the severity of maiming so varied across cultures. Why did the customs to control women seem less ferocious in Europe than in Asia and North Africa? The spike heel and even the chastity belt seem mild compared to suttee, foot-binding, and clitoridectomy.

Goody (1983) suggests that the milder constraints on the behavior of European women were an unexpected consequence of measures taken by the Roman Catholic Church to induce adherents to leave it their wealth. For example, the church reduced a person's number of close relatives by abolishing adoption and close-cousin marriages. Some of the measures clearly benefited women as well. The church banned child marriages and often gave women the right to inherit land. A woman who entered a convent could later leave the land she inherited to the church. The assorted measures worked. About a third of the productive land in France was in church hands by the end of the seventh century. In German lands, northern France, and Italy, the church owned twice as much land in the ninth as the eighth century (Goody 1983:103).

Subsistence Technology and Human Health

Permanent settlements became possible when the domestication of various kinds of wild grains enabled farmers to produce enough surplus food to support the political and social activities that characterize village or urban life. The upside of city living included spacious housing as well as the flourishing of arts that tends to occur when well-heeled patrons can support talented writers, composers, musicians, painters, and architects. The downside is that crowded living conditions created a problem in the disposal of human and animal wastes. The aroma of rotting sewage in urban areas may surpass the imagination of moderns who take safe drinking water and flush toilets for granted. Even so, the worst feature of city life was not the stink of mammal wastes but rather the effect of the ubiquity of sewage on human health. Only a few generations ago even Queen Victoria's husband became a victim of "bad drains" in Buckingham Palace.

Permanent human settlements resulted in higher rates of infection and stunted growth. Urban life was bad for elites and worse for ordinary folk (Cohen 1989). Nomad foragers had been as tall as contemporary affluent peoples in the economically advanced nation-states (Eaton, Eaton, and Konner 1999:231). Compared with the height of their forager ancestors, farmers shrank in size, for the typical diet of a peasant or serf family in an economy based on grain contained far too much bread and not nearly enough meat, fruits, and vegetables to promote human growth. Braudel (1978:130) described the standard diet in early modern Europe as consisting of bread, more bread, and gruel. Abundant evidence shows that humans are ill adapted to a grain diet (Larsen 2000:231).

For one thing, a grain-based diet worsens dental health. Nomad foods required heavy-duty chewing, which increases the size of jaw muscle and bone. Grain-based foods need little chewing (and their sugar content hastens the process of dental decay). Over time, jaw muscle and bone become smaller owing to lack of sufficient use. Teeth, which were more under genetic control, stayed about the same size. The ensuing discrepancy in size of jaw and teeth gave rise to the malocclusion and decay that provide a good living for contemporary orthodontists (see Larsen 2000:209).

The most important consequence of a grain diet is its worsening of the problems of disease transmission and poor sanitation posed by large permanent settlements. Poorly fed people resist disease with difficulty. Life was especially hard for newly weaned infants, who lost the immune protection of maternal milk amidst a plethora of pathogens.

Parental Resources and Child Care

In foraging communities, each woman nursed her own infant because the infant could digest no food but human milk, and parents lacked the resources to hire another woman to feed their infant. Parents generally left a deformed infant and at least one of a set of twins alone to die. In very hard times, even normal infants could suffer the same fate, for in some circumstances the parents had no other choice.

By contrast, the pyramidal pattern of stratification made possible by the plow highlighted the differential allocation of resources among families. Rich parents could capture nutritional resources for their children that otherwise might have been more evenly distributed. The ensuing patterns of infant care illustrate the painful decisions that poor parents had to make in allocating resources to their own children. Below, I discuss three modes of infant nourishment that illustrate the effects of the modes of social stratification that followed upon the invention of agriculture: wet-nursing, hand-feeding, and abandonment.

Wet-Nursing

A wet nurse is a lactating woman paid to suckle a child not her own. The practice could involve the death of the wet-nurse's own child. The huge drain on the maternal system made it unlikely that a woman had milk for more than one child over a prolonged period (Wood 1994:17, 204; Stini 1985:203). The infant whose mother had died or become too disabled to lactate was in a real fix, but its chances improved if its parents were rich enough to hire a lactating woman.

The use of a wet nurse usually stemmed from a parental preference to free a wife for other activities; very few women are unable to lactate. UNICEF estimates that 97 percent of women are capable of giving milk (Jolly 1999:330). Wealthy parents more often than not bought their child's life with the life of another (Fildes 1986). Well established in Greek and Roman times when slave women were available, wet-nursing became common among upper class Europeans by the medieval period (Fildes 1986:98).

The protoindustrial period spread the demand for wet-nursing across a wider segment of the class structure and, as we shall soon see, the rate of infant abandonment also increased the demand. Though economists usually ignore the value of maternal time in computing the cost of breast-feeding (Butz 1977), ordinary women seem to sense it. Wet-nursing became much more common in protoindustrial Europe when the increased availability of wage work raised the opportunity cost of prolonged suckling. For example, at a time when male wages were low and many wives worked in the burgeoning silk industry in France, parents shipped a majority of Lyonnais infants to villages in nearby areas (Garden 1957:122, 351). Parisian parents sent an even higher proportion of infants away. The death rates of the wet nurses' own infants were extremely high in the seventeenth to the early nineteenth century in Europe (Fildes 1988:193).

Wet-nursing has been studied in the United States far less than in Europe, according to a recent and detailed study (Golden 2001:3). European scholars can turn to the archives of church and state, as each institution was deeply involved in caring for abandoned infants and placing them with wet nurses. By contrast, American religious and secular authorities exerted no systematic oversight over abandoned infants, a fact that set American social historians on a different path.

At its core, wet nursing involved a nearly untraceable interaction of a woman, her own child, and the one she was hired to feed (Golden 2001:7). Women became wet nurses primarily to earn money, though for some women wet nursing was a way to reject responsibility for their own infants while capitalizing on the most valuable commodity yielded by childbirth: human milk. The words of the wet nurses are lost to historians.

Hand-Feeding

The hand-feeding of a grain-based pap in case of maternal death or incapability goes back 4,000 years, as indicated by the utensils discovered by archeologists (Fildes 1986:262). In some areas, newborns received pap alone even when the mother could presumably provide milk, as in some Bavarian villages in the early modern period (Knodel 1988). In late medieval Iceland infants received cow's milk. The only infants who received human milk were those of women too poor to keep a cow (Hastrup 1985). As would be expected, the infants given cow's milk had extremely high death rates while the ones who suckled human milk were considerably more likely to survive. The rationale for these seemingly risky and irrational practices remains obscure. Hastrup (1985) attributed the behavior to beliefs that emphasized the importance of the cow. Fildes (1986:264) thinks that in a cold climate with high standards of maternal care and cleanliness, the five-year survival rate of hand-fed and breast-fed infants may have differed little because the postweaning death rates were high whatever the child's age at weaning. However, Wray's (1977:206) historical study reports that a diet of human milk instead of pap nearly doubled child survival rates.

A related practice, early weaning to a grain-based pap, may have enabled a mother to work away from her child. In nineteenth century Russia the practice permitted mothers to do field work (Ransel 1988:269). In Nepal today, mothers cease nursing their three-year-olds when women's work load rises during the monsoon season. A diet of leftover table scraps under conditions of high temperature and humidity ensures that the death rate of three-year-old weanlings will be higher than that of the younger children who are breast-fed (Panter-Brick 1992b). The early feeding of infants with some kind of pap plausibly enabled slave mothers to work away from their children in the American South, but I have found no studies on this topic.

Infant Abandonment

In nonliterate cultures, the abandoning of infants tended to occur when food was too scarce to feed another child. In literate societies, the major reason for abandonment was much the same but the practice was also used to save the mother's honor were she unmarried and the infant's death less a certainty. A few infants lived through it.

Parents abandoned children in great number in Europe from the end of the Hellenistic period to the end of the Middle Ages without the mediation of public institutions (Boswell

1988:428). According to dos Guimaraes Sa (2000:28), foundlings increasingly were cared for in the foundling hospitals that emerged across Europe, first in Italy, then in Spain, Portugal, and France from the thirteenth to the seventeenth century, and to northern and central Europe in the second half of the eighteenth century. The hospitals encouraged an extensive market in wet-nursing, resulting in a hierarchy of wet nurses. The foundling hospitals usually hired the poorest women with the least milk.

In protoindustrial Europe, in a period when male wages were low, abandonment was associated with women's opportunities for wage work, for the required activities typically precluded the suckling of an infant. In 1780, for example, parents gave up perhaps 8,000 of the 30,000 infants born in Paris (Braudel 1979:491). Newspapers report incidences of child abandonment even today.

In Italy, the rate of infant abandonment rose sharply after the Roman Catholic Church tightened its rules in response to the Protestant Reformation (Kertzer 1993). Lest a child die before a priest could baptize it, local officials urged the mother, usually unmarried, to hand it over to a well-developed church bureaucracy. A rural woman working as an urban live-in servant was the most likely parent, for she was in a weak position to persuade the infant's father to marry her. Whether wet-nursed or fed by hand, few of these foundlings survived childhood (Kertzer 1993:138). The foundling home in Florence, which continues to accept abandoned children, housed 69 of them in 1994, the majority born out of wedlock (Viazzo, Bortolotto, and Zanotti 2000:71).

As cities grew, poor sanitation and urban squalor continued to make human milk optimal for infant survival. In rural Third World countries (as in eighteenth-century London), Fildes (1986:401) reports that up to 70 percent of infants die before their second birthday. Many nineteenth-century documents report death rates of 80 to 90 percent for infants who were not breast-fed (Cone 1981:12; see also Preston and Haines 1991).

The Advent of Modern Sanitation

By 1910, the discovery of the germ theory of disease and related discoveries and inventions that date from the 1880s made the bottle almost as safe as the breast in areas with modern public sanitation (Huber 1990). The presence of a literate female population probably helped. Safe drinking water and unspoiled food had more to do with the decline of gastro-intestinal diseases spread by contaminated water and food than did medical intervention, because physicians had no access to therapeutic measures of value until about 1950 (McKeown 1976:54). Nonetheless, medical research was highly significant in bringing about the series of changes that led to the fading away of the ancient custom of frequent and prolonged breastfeeding.

By 1950, bottle feeding was widespread in the West (Stuart-Macadam 1995:28). Today about half of U.S. newborns begin on the breast. Only seven percent are nursed more than 12 months (Potts and Short 1999:268). The ancient mode of breastfeeding is clearly a thing of the past in America. Bottle feeding has become more of an issue among many well-educated women who are aware of the benefits of human milk for infants (Rothman 1993).

Both demographers and health workers agree that the immunological content of human milk together with the avoidance of unsafe water and food lower infant mortality and morbidity (Vitzthum 1997:244). Reports on the benefits of breast milk generally try to distinguish the effects on both morbidity and mortality. Ample data report that breast-fed infants suffer less than do bottle-fed ones from a variety of ailments in both modern and traditional economies. The data for modern economies are hard to interpret because in the infant's first year breast milk often is supplemented by formula and solid food at some time (Lawrence 1994:28). In areas that lack adequate public sanitation, mortality is much higher for bottle-fed infants than breast-fed ones. In modern economies, it is not clear that mortality rates differ for bottle-fed and breast-fed ones. Bottle-fed infants clearly suffer more ailments in the course of growing up, but so far as I have been able to discover, the bottle-fed are as likely as the breast-fed to live long enough to reproduce.

Where clean water is rare, bottle feeding remains deadly. For example, when poor women massively entered wage work in Northeast Brazil in the early 1940s, breast-feeding declined from 96 to 40 percent and continued to fall despite very high rates of infant death (Scheper-Hughes 1992:317; Scheper-Hughes and Sargent 1998:5). Despite the effect on infant mortality, economic development lowers the rate of breastfeeding owing to the expansion of market opportunities for women (Da Vanzo 1988; Palloni and Tienda 1985). Worldwide, mothers have tended to behave as if frequent and prolonged breastfeeding had a high opportunity cost, even when the effects on their infants' lives are clear and severe.

Chapter Six

The Future of Gender Inequality

THE PURPOSE OF THIS BOOK is to explain why research on the gendering of human institutions requires the use of biodata in order to explain the emergence of particular patterns. I focus on lactation, for social scientists (as well as the general public) are largely unaware of the constraints the ancient mode placed on women's activities. A very frequent and prolonged pattern benefited both mother and child but the mother alone bore the costs, for breastfeeding limited her to activities she could manage while toting an infant or parking it nearby. Infant need for human milk thus shored up a sexual division of labor that began to erode only after advances in applied science so increased the safety of so-called artificial feeding that survival rates of bottle- and breast-fed infants became much the same.

The most important consequence of very frequent and prolonged lactation was that women could take no part in governance and military affairs, which were closely linked until a few centuries ago when the ties were eroded by a series of events soon to be described. Absence from politics and warfare barred women from competing in the activities typically rewarded with the most prestige and power.

In this chapter I show how the reciprocal effects of common literacy, technology, behavior, and belief set the stage for the rise in women's mainstream participation during the twentieth century. After noting the sex differences in physiology that mark our species, I discuss why one of these remains largely unknown and unanalyzed in the social sciences. I then go to the bottom line: Will the reciprocal effects of applied science, human behavior, and shared beliefs ultimately degender human institutions? In our species, physiological sex differences remain unchanged, but technology has profoundly altered their social effects. At the microlevel of events, individuals are well aware that their lives differ from those of their great-grandparents, but at the macrolevel, some of these changes have yet to seep into a common view of reality that integrates biology and social structure.

Physiological Sex Differences

Two kinds of physiological differences mark the sexes in our species. One is categorical. A given quality in one sex is absent in the other. For example, no man can bear a child. The other is statistical: Men tend to be larger and stronger than women are but some women are larger and stronger than most men. The only categorical sex differences are those of reproduction. The others are statistical. I first discuss a categorical difference, lactation, that has received remarkably little study in the social sciences.

Breastfeeding that is very frequent and prolonged is a hidden structure that divides premodern from modern women, upon whom applied science has bestowed other options. In a profound change that has received little comment from the pundits who analyze human affairs, a mode of lactation that evolved among primates over millions of years began to erode late in the nineteenth century as a result of events brought into being by urban living and the industrial revolution. A preference for bottle feeding an infant with cow's milk crossed class and ethnic lines among all women (Wolf 2001:9, 3). Commercial firms advertised items intended for infant diet, some of which were recommended by physicians. Even mothers who nursed their infants began to schedule fewer feeds per day over a significantly shorter period of time.

The preference for breastfeeding had its ups and downs in twentieth century America (Wolf 2001). Early on, higher status mothers tended to prefer bottle feeding, for they had come to see breastfeeding as an old-fashioned mode preferred primarily by women immigrants from poor countries. Later in the century, well-educated mothers breast-fed more often than did other women, for they understood its benefits for the infant and had the resources to practice what the experts preached. Compared to the ancient mode, however, the pattern adopted by young mothers was less frequent and prolonged, more suited to a schedule that (especially with the help of a breast pump and an airline ticket) let a mother spend goodly chunks of time away from her infant.

The change in the mode of infant feeding in advanced economies was apparently taken for granted, perhaps because twentieth century interest in the female breast tended to obscure its utility in infant nutrition. When a new wave of the women's movement emerged in the 1970s, the facts about frequent and prolonged lactation were virtually unknown. Late in the twentieth century new findings in biology supplemented by field work in anthropology reported that human infants had been fed far more often and over a longer period of time than anyone had supposed.

By contrast with the topic of breastfeeding, the statistical sex differences that give males an edge in size and strength are well known. Persons generously endowed with these attributes have an advantage in activities that involve coercion. Whether or not humans are innately predisposed to violence is an issue from which military historians have prudently distanced themselves (Keegan 1996:50). Research in biology, ethnology, and psychology has been contentious because most authors find it hard to discuss aggression unaggressively (Eibl-Eibesfeldt 1979:6). Contemporary biologists (see Chapter 5) see human aggression as a response to overcrowding when resources are too meager to support a population (Wilson 1996:64).

The male advantage in aggression is usually taken for granted. However, the one comprehensive survey of recent research on the male edge in size and strength that I have found, that of political scientist Joshua Goldstein (2001:182), upsets the common wisdom: No statistical sex difference adequately explains why women were excluded from warfare. Goldstein (2001:250) (see also Maccoby 1998) holds that individual variation and sex overlap should have enabled a nontrivial minority of women to engage in combat even though several factors that tend to favor men could have added up to a huge mandate for men in combat roles: greater average size and strength, subtle brain adaptation for rough and tumble play, a somewhat different orientation to competitive hierarchies, and a tendency toward sex segregation in childhood. Yet, the four elements do not combine additively so much as they overlap. The women who make the best soldiers tend to be those who are relatively strong, aggressive, spatially adept, rough, and competitive.

As levels of the hormone testosterone clearly separate the sexes, differential levels have been used to explain male superiority in aggressive activities, but these claims are wrong. The relationship of testosterone and aggression is complex (Goldstein 2001:148–56). Intermale aggression, the most often studied, is related most to the status hierarchies elicited by breeding competition. The results seem not to apply to other forms of aggression, including war (Goldstein 2001:148). The claim that testosterone levels explain women's absence from combat was unsupported (see also Mazur and Booth 1998). Testosterone does not cause existing patterns of aggression, rather, it amplifies them. Effects on human male-female dominance or competition have yet to be studied. Evidence connects testosterone with aggression only as part of a feedback loop, and the stronger causal links run from social behavior to hormone levels.

No evidence supports the idea that only males can form the bonds that inspire group loyalty. Females bond as easily as do males. Nor are most wars won by the side with larger and stronger soldiers. Military historians stress the importance of strategy, fighting spirit, discipline, intelligence, and quality of weaponry in battle outcomes. The one war that the United States lost was to an army whose members tended to be shorter and weaker than American males.

Though the ten percent of women who are the largest and strongest would make good warriors, the only well-documented case of a large-scale female combat unit that functioned for a long period (the 1700s into the 1900s) as part of a standing army is that of the Kingdom of Dahomey (now Benin) in West Africa (Goldstein 2001:60; see also Goody 1971:52). Large, strong males were in short supply owing to a slave trade that sold off huge numbers of able-bodied men. Herskovits (1938:85, 88) claims that women, who were a tenth to a third of the army, had as much or more courage than did men. They were celibate or, if pregnant, were killed. Fierce as wounded gorillas, they could endure great fatigue; in this part of Africa, women did most of the work.

Goldstein (2001:413) concluded that no one knows how to end war, equalize gender, or undo the links of gender and war. Yet, complex systems hold many possibilities. In a multicausal feedback system, leverage at various points affects an entire system, a point I take up later.

It has been unfortunate that research on the biology of human sex differences continues to fall on deaf ears in the social sciences and humanities. To avoid the racism of nineteenth-century anthropology, Boas early on had urged colleagues to emphasize the primacy of culture over race as a cause of group differences. Feminists later intensified the rejection in the 1970s because biological research was so often used to justify male supremacy. Their rejection was soon intensified by a wave of postmodernist theory that swept across the humanities and those areas of social science that engaged in descriptive research. Postmodernism took a dim view of the eighteenth-century Enlightenment, rationalism, and causal analysis. Proponents of postmodernism in sociology typically rejected biology outright.

By contrast, quantitative analysts, especially in sociology, did not so much reject biology as ignore it. The study of social stratification shifted from macrolevel analysis of class structure to microanalysis of survey data in order to reveal the extent of generational transmission of educational and occupational attainment. The so-called attainment model attracted some of the best minds in the discipline. Its focus was narrow but its answers were precise. Most of the studies excluded women. Those that did not revealed that the lifetime earnings of a woman college graduate resembled those of a male high school graduate because many females had left the labor market upon marriage or especially after childbirth, never to return.

Occasional attempts were made to alert sociologists to the importance of biology in explanations of women's status. For example, Alice Rossi (1983) claimed in her presidential address to the American Sociological Association that sex differences in hormones produced psychological tendencies that affected the division of parental labor, but most of the feminists in the audience tuned the message out. Feminist theory, Marxism, mainstream social science, and even women's health studies paid scant attention to the biological components of human behavior (Rossi 1987:73), and feminists as a body largely neglected the topic of lactation (van Esterik 1989:4).

Hindsight suggests that sociological theories of gender stratification suffered most from the neglect of a large and richly suggestive body of research conducted by women and men in physical anthropology and primatology. This research, which undermined the idea that science supports biological determinism, included such scholars as Peter Ellison (1994), Frans de Waal (1982), Sarah Hrdy (1981), Jane Lancaster (1991), Barbara Smuts (1995), Carol Worthman (1993), Richard Wrangham (1994), and many others.

Instead, feminist interest in human biology centered on the social construction of women's health issues such as the so-called medicalization (medical control) of pregnancy and lactation. Recent work has focused on the effect of human milk on infant health (e.g., Golden 2001; Wolf 2001), and on ideologies of breastfeeding by "race" and class (Blum 1999). The idea that frequent and prolonged lactation might relate women's control over their activities to their place in the social order lay beyond the purview of the scholars who conducted this research.

Technology and Human Behavior

Below, I show how technological change set the stage for women to play an increasing part in activities outside the household, though technology neither structured the play nor dictated the details of the script. Women wrote the lines for themselves. New technologies only permit change. Humans themselves must alter their behaviors, beliefs, and, ultimately, their institutions in order to bring it about.

To understand the effect of the industrial revolution on gendered inequality one must grasp the distinction between a physiological sex difference and the social effects of that difference. For example, new technologies enabled humans to augment their labor with machines that increased worker output without changing the physiological limitations of human muscular strength. Similarly, applied science made it easier for women to limit their births and alter the mode of infant feeding even though the physiology of human reproduction is about the same today as in the Paleolithic period. New technologies can alter the social effects of physiological attributes even though the attributes themselves remain unchanged.

Few theorists sensed that for the first time in human history, women could begin to avoid the constraints that had shaped the lives of their sex for thousands of years. The problem was the confusion of the social effects of physiological constraints with the constraints themselves, perhaps because change occurred so rapidly. The pace of social change is infinitely faster than that of biological evolution, for humans themselves invent the stimuli that spur transformation. Fertility declined when children began to become more an economic burden than an asset to their parents. The reduction was achieved by using the technique of withdrawal, later, the condom (Kirk 1968:344). By 1880, an effective condom was available in England, though it was very expensive (see Huber and Spitze 1983:31). By the 1960s, when the introduction of "the pill" gave women a nearly foolproof way to separate reproduction and sexual pleasure, U.S. fertility fell a little below replacement, and some European rates fell well below that level.

The combined effects of declining fertility and the increasing safety of bottle feeding enabled large numbers of women to take advantage of an expanding number of clerical and service jobs. The proportion of American women working for pay is now close to that of men,[1] and the proportion of women in positions of power also rose, albeit with deliberate speed. The rise in the number of well-educated employed women increased their awareness of the sex gap in attainment and reward, and set the stage for a new feminist movement (Huber 1976).

There are no clear answers as to how far these trends toward gender equality may go now that the constraints on women have become attenuated. They may continue until women's social and economic status roughly equals that of men or they could be deflected in another direction before they jell into a pattern that could pass for equality. Predicting the future is risky. Variables multiply. Unimaginable inventions open new vistas and disasters cancel old ones. Crucial to the future of any trend is the extent of change in public opinion.

Public Opinion

The most durable social trends involve the interplay of technology, behavior, and belief. Most often, technological change affects behavior and behavioral change in turn affects belief. Though changes in belief generally lag behind, belief and behavior tend to become congruent over time. People are more comfortable when they think that what they do is in fact what they ought to be doing.

Some beliefs are hard to change. When a belief shores up the privileges of the powerful, it may persist even when the factors that brought it into being have weakened. In the United States, one of the most religiously traditional countries in Christendom, fundamentalist beliefs continue to influence attitudes about human origins and the role of women (Lipset 1989:191). The ideology of male dominance expressed in the sacred writings of Jews, Christians, and Muslims remains entrenched in the popular mind, owing to the tendency of groups to preserve their own interests and to human tendency to see biological attributes as permanent because they change so imperceptibly.

The so-called industrial revolution, a congeries of discoveries and inventions that spread worldwide from its beginnings in Northwest Europe, exemplifies the most rapid speed of social change known to date. The labor movement that it spawned when erstwhile peasants, serfs, and slaves massively entered urban labor markets was better known as the men's movement. Women had little part in it, for they were seen primarily as competitors for male jobs (Huber and Spitze 1981). The demands of ordinary men for the right to vote and to a fair share of goods dominated nineteenth-century politics in Europe and North America, and spread to other parts of the world as displaced rural workers migrated to cities.

Early in the twentieth century, women's rising level of education similarly spawned a movement that focused on the legal, political, and economic rights of middle-class women. Later in the century, a new wave of that movement echoed the nineteenth-century men's movement that had emerged when masses of rural men sought work in urban settings. In the period after World War II, masses of married women entered the labor market to stay until retirement. Women responded to an increase in their discretionary time, their level of education, and the number of white collar clerical and service jobs available. A rather brief period thus witnessed profound change in the longstanding social effects of pregnancy and lactation on the kind of work women did.

When the political ideas of the 1970s began to seep into academia, the intellectual scene was dominated by scholars who had long taken male domination for granted as a fact of human life so obvious that it needed no explanation. The reasons given, if any, focused on female reproduction and male size and strength, though a few authors noted a male tendency to bond in groups that excluded women.

Yet, the lack of analysis left questions. Had women tended to be larger and stronger than men, would lactation have barred them from warfare? What are the effects of size and strength on domination among men? Do larger, stronger men dominate shorter, weaker ones? Do young men dominate old ones? Why or why not? And why did women long take no part in military or political affairs? Such questions lay fallow until the second wave of the women's movement sounded a wakeup call. Below, I characterize the output of those disciplines that have studied warfare, and then provide a chronological and substantive account of the rise in the efficiency of killing humans.

History and Social Science on Warfare

Most accounts of the use of force are the work of historians, for the huge literature in military history extends from ancient to modern times while the slender output of the social sciences goes back only a century. Women were nearly invisible in the activities that interested historians. Chieftains, kings, warriors (and the historians themselves) were men to a man. Save for the exceptions in classical accounts,[2] women warriors emerged only in revolutionary settings when fighters were badly needed. The advent of social history and rise in the number of women historians effected no change. Social historians typically left the study of warfare to others, and feminists tended to abhor war and shun the study of militarism.

The analysis of warfare was long integral to political science under the rubric of international relations. Till very recently, the absence of women was as unquestioned in analyses of international diplomacy as it had been in military history.

Few anthropologists and even fewer sociologists have written about warfare. The standard texts in those disciplines have no chapters on war (Andreski 1992:3; Hamilton 1999), though a subset of anthropologists initiated the study of war among nonliterate people early in the 1900s (see below). According to Moskos (1971), sociological research on the military dates from World War II, but the position of women was not examined. Janowitz (1960) said little about them in *The Professional Soldier;* he thought women had had little impact on the organizational climate in World War II (Janowitz 1971:417–30).

Stanislav Andreski's (1968) comparative Weberian perspective on military organization and society exemplified the strength of sociological analysis. Unaware of the constraints of lactation on women's activities, Andreski (1992:12) held that women's inferiority stemmed ultimately from their being weaker in combat. His use of the comparative method demonstrates why Weberian analysis has been so fruitful. Andreski (1968:268) concluded that the more militaristic a society, the lower the status of its women. To my knowledge, this analysis of women and war is unsurpassed in the sociological literature.

Though the work of two British feminists and a semanticist (Marshall, Ogden, and Florence 1987 [1915]) marked an early beginning, feminist literature on women and warfare began to emerge in the social sciences only in the 1970s when a rise in the number of women scholars was coupled with the creation of a voluntary force that spurred a huge increase in the number of women in the services (Goldman 1973:146; Holm 1992:246). This research documents in detail the wishful thinking and facile rationalization that tend to accompany ethnocentric efforts to suppress competition. The writers who held that women soldiers would be the ruination of military institutions seem to have taken lessons from the nineteenth- and twentieth-century scholars who vigorously opposed women's entry into higher education, law, and medicine.

Primitive War

Anthropologists, who use the word "primitive" to describe aspects of nonliterate cultures, saw hunting and warfare as a male monopoly and took men's need to defend their group for granted (Davie 1929:45). Primitive wars were marked by weak command and lack of adequate supply lines, hence they were generally brief. Warriors were specialized only by age. Unlike "civilized" war, primitive war was long thought to be a largely ceremonial affair, akin to a modern football game (Turney-High 1945:75; but see Vayda 1976).

Studies of warfare among nonliterate peoples rose sharply from 1960 to 1980, stimulated by research in behavioral ecology (Otterbein 1999). Sociobiology provided the theoretical basis. Humans must solve the same ecological problems as do other species if they are to reproduce (Low, Clarke, and Lockridge 1992). Ecologists came to agree that scarce resources often led to war among primates, including our human ancestors (Ember and Ember 1992). As world historian William McNeill (1982:23) put it, getting enough to eat has always been the central task of human life and remains a perpetual problem for most persons even today.

Very recently, new archeological data from the American Southwest indicated that primitive warfare had been an extremely bloody business (LeBlanc 1999; Lambert 2000). The severity of prehistoric massacres wiped out entire tribes. High death rates resulted from the frequency of battles and raids, the proportion of men in combat, and the terrible treatment of women and children (Keeley 1996:93). Whether this mode of warfare prevailed in other ecological areas has not yet been demonstrated.

Primitive warfare separated male and female interests, for the sharing of combat roles spawns high group loyalty. Soldiers fight not for king and country but for friends, as do their chimpanzee cousins. Military training has always been designed as an intensely emotional experience that welds men into a unit, each loyal to the others (Potts and Short 1999:199). In turn, absence from warrior cliques barred women from the quasimilitary in-groups that dominated political institutions after the invention of metallurgy so altered warfare that elites could control far larger areas in richer societies that were more stratified socially.

The Invention of Metallurgy

Primitive war ended in Eurasia, Africa, and the Americas with the invention of metallurgy. The use of metal weapons made killing more efficient. In this respect we humans have made huge progress. In regard to instruments of torture there has been little change. Advanced methods were known at the time of Hammurabi and little improvement has been made since (Andreski 1968:36).

According to military historian Ernest Dupuy (1980:1), bronze implements were used as early 3,000 BCE in Crete. The use of iron weapons can be dated to about 1,500 BCE and of horses, around 1,000 BCE. The first battle in recorded history took place at Megiddo in Palestine in 1,469 BCE. The tribes of Palestine and Syria had revolted against a young Egyptian pharaoh, but he won an overwhelming victory.

The technology needed to make metal weapons, like the use of horses, increased not only the efficiency but also the cost of war. In turn, the high cost of producing arms and equipment tended to restrict arms-bearing to elites (Andreski 1969:38). Eurasian cavalry included lesser nobles with enough wealth to own horses and supply themselves with armor and weapons. The elite striking force of most armies consisted of a contingent of chariots in which great nobles or members of royal families charged into battle (Dupuy 1980:2–3).

Better weapons induce more complexity in political organization. War had been rare for most of human time on earth because crowding was minimal, one person to a square mile. Anthropologists Allen Johnson and Timothy Earle (1987:58, 245) report that war became more common when population pressure spurred the formation of local groups five to ten times larger than a typical family to act on issues of food storage and defense. When a chief could institutionalize adequate control over central storage, large-scale technology, external trade, and warfare, he could organize an entire region.

Though few social science problems are less accessible to direct research than the origin of political institutions (Fried 1979:76), the military was perhaps the key element in the formation of large-scale political institutions such as complex chiefdoms and, later, states (Earle 1997:105). The association between military power and a paramount chief is unarguable because autonomous units do not yield their independence unless they must. That there should still be so much uncertainty about such a basic step in the history of human governance demonstrates how little hard thinking has gone into it (Carneiro 1998:19, 22).

The invention of metallurgy enabled political and military elites to establish huge kingdoms and empires whose eventual collapse led to a mode of social organization known as feudalism. The collapse of the Roman Empire about 1,500 years ago marked the beginnings of feudalism in Europe. The dissolution of the Empire paralleled a decline in military leadership, ingenuity, and discipline that ushered in a new era. Armed force, vigorous and violent, was used with little systematic doctrine or imagination during a period of squalid butchery (Dupuy 1980:41).

The absence of centralized control opened the door to hordes of robbers who made roads unsafe to travel in the so-called Middle Ages of European history. The protection (and oppression) of peasants, serfs, and slaves fell to local politicos rather than to the Roman army. Landlords with ample resources outfitted crews of knights who plundered the locals but protected them from the predations of the knightly thugs who served the lord of another demesne down the road. The European ruling class remained a military one to the end of the old order in France (Keegan 1987:4).

The Intimacy of Governance and Warfare

The huge historical literature that deals with premodern war and conquest makes one point clear: Conquest necessarily involved politics.[3] Leaders had to organize some portion of a population for armed migration into another area. Winners had to pacify losers in order to dun them for tribute and taxes, as when successive waves of migrants from the Asian steppes overran Europe before, during, and after the decline of Roman hegemony (Heather 1996) or when Muslims expanded their hegemony from its base in West Asia to an area that extended from Southwest Europe to East Asia (Lewis 1995). Following conquest, political stability is integral to the infusion of resources into a system from the outside. We-they distinctions that explain and justify unequal relations between winners and losers cover the process of pacification with a convenient ideological cloak.

The constraints of lactation alone would have excluded women from the politics of pacification owing to lack of fit between combat readiness and frequent suckling, but it is likely that male ethnocentrism as expressed in the masculine military ideology described by Stiehm (1989) and Enloe (1993) also played a part. This form of ethnocentrism is akin to what Collins et al. (1993) called sexual politics, the tendency of all-male groups to become solidaristic around masculine erotic identity. In humans, the availability of language enables males to devise ideologies of male dominance/female subordination and male supremacy/female inferiority that explain and justify women's secondary status (Smuts 1995).

Collins et al. (1993) hold that the most striking effect of sexual politics is on the gendered ranking that separates male and female spheres and leads to a dual status system and the gendering of production. The competitive structure of the sexual politics elicits sexual aggression and the stereotyping of women as sexual objects. In hoe cultures, male segregation in militarized men's houses spawned highly antagonistic gender ideologies. In agrarian states dominated by military aristocracies, lower class women were sexual plunder. In modern polities, military prostitution has been seen as a matter of national security (Moon 1997). The demilitarizing of daily life under the bureaucratic state reduces the extreme features of male sexual coercion, but all-male groups nonetheless continue to harbor a sexually aggressive culture that is evidenced in competitive athletics, gang violence, fraternity carousing, and military institutions (Collins et al. 1993).

Ethnocentrism stems from functional relations that reflect group interests. There is no serious challenge to its basic tenet: the higher the conflict of interest, the greater the level of ethnocentrism (Levine and Campbell 1972:222). Biologists have shown how the conflict of male and female interests begin with those of reproduction, and then tend to spread pervasively into aspects of daily life. When ascribed statuses such as sex and race are used as axes of social organization, the phenotypic markers and social warp and woof they provide make for effective social control (Hechter 1987:186; see also Crenshaw and Robison 2005). Visible markers permit the identification of individuals who are classified as members of a particular category. The ethnocentrism of top dogs spawns a set of beliefs that permit the control of underdogs.

Male control of decisionmaking enabled them to regulate marriage, inheritance, and property rights such that these institutions embodied the self-interest of elite males. For nonelite males, service as warriors deepened the gendering of interests, for the training that both primitive warriors and modern soldiers undergo instills a near mystical devotion to the group.[4] Conviction based upon deeply experienced emotion is then reinforced by a rational notion neatly in accord with common sense: Loyalty to comrades on the battlefield maximizes one's chances of survival.

After the French Revolution, the larger nation-states increasingly used universal conscription to raise armies and navies big enough to wage the kind of war technology had made possible for relatively rich countries when they hoped to acquire overseas empires. To offset the chances of early death, universal conscription became a carrot that offered the reward of full rights to all men who served, and the idea took root that only armed males had the rights of full citizenship (Keegan 1996:233). Military service thus infused the modern concept of citizenship from its beginnings (Kerber 1998:236).

Men monopolized warfare down to modern times. The constraints of childrearing would have sufficed to exclude women but the male advantage in size and strength and the fact that large and strong women could be warriors only if they remained celibate doubtless played a part, as did male ethnocentrism and the socialization of both sexes.

Historically, the male monopoly on coercion has been inextricably intertwined with the power to make and enforce laws. Warfare and politics, like so-called Siamese twins, could not easily be separated. Successful military command, readily convertible into political leadership, enabled elite males to erect a legal edifice that would preserve their privileges. Conquering heroes and their minions have had first dibs on political control in the days of Joshua, Alexander the Great, Julius Caesar, and Frederick the Great, to say nothing of Napoleon and even Fidel Castro. The monarch commanded his nation's military forces, and his normal dress was a military uniform (Dupuy 1980:138).

Conjoined Twins Asunder

After the invention of settled agriculture, political and military leadership became as one. Yet, new events can set asunder what historical circumstance first joined. Beginning three or four hundred years ago in the protomodern countries of Western Europe, the breakdown of communal land tenure and production systems as a result of population pressure elicited social innovations such as private property, wage labor, and inheritance laws, all of which had evolved well before industrialism (Crenshaw and Robison 2005).

At some period after the invention of the printing press, the strong linkage of military and political leadership became increasingly attenuated in nation-states that had the means and the will to require universal education. Though war remains a continuation of politics by other means as Clausewitz claimed (Browning 2002:44), eminent generals now experience more difficulty than formerly in using military success as a stepping stone to high political position in the Western democracies. It is much the same for politicians who aspire to control military affairs. It doesn't happen often in a well-established democracy and when it does, it usually does not last long. Hitler strutted about in military uniform and told the high command what to do, but his thousand-year Reich lasted little more than a decade.

The separation of the major entry tracks to leadership in war and politics was a consequence of new forms of governance made possible and also (one hopes) inevitable by a rise in common literacy that followed upon the invention of the printing press. Common mastery of the ability to read and the proliferation of printed matter enabled a better informed public to figure out what political leaders were really up to and, if needed, to raise enough commotion to induce kings, ministers, and their minions to head in another direction. It is in countries that have thus far been unable to provide basic education universally to boys and especially to girls that generals too often convert military success into political power and presidents become dictators who control the military establishment.

Universal suffrage thus became a means of conferring a halo of legitimacy on political institutions, as evidenced by its use even in polities that generally are defined as dictatorships.

Though the military route to political leadership remains an option in polities with low literacy rates, military elites in Europe and North America have lost the political clout and charisma that was once theirs. If erstwhile generals hope to attain high political office, they are obliged to discuss their stands on issues that ordinary citizens care about. To court an electorate successfully, a general is best endowed with a temperament more given to persuasion than to barking out orders that must be obeyed without question.

By contrast, military leaders have no such obligation to those they command. Though the American experience in Iraq indicates a need for stronger incentives to promote well-calculated risk-taking among the officers at lower ranks (Asch and Hosek 2004:17; see also Dupuy 1980:337–43), it is hard to see how military decisions, especially in combat situations, could ever be effective without a clear-cut hierarchy of command. In organizations that require participants to put their lives on the line under conditions that are often close to chaos, a leader must be free to make decisions that will be obeyed without question. A town meeting is ineffective on a battlefield.

The separation of military and political leadership highlights another difference in the two arenas. Military institutions tend to avoid the recruitment of smaller and weaker persons. By contrast, persons do not succeed in the political arena on the basis of size, strength, and aggressive proclivities, for political skills depend much more on other attributes. Among old world primates, individuals who often aggress against others to maintain dominance are typically in the process of dropping in the hierarchy; individuals in stable dominant positions tend to rely on bluffing and psychological intimidation (Altmann et al. 1995:688). Similarly, larger and stronger males do not necessarily dominate shorter and weaker ones (Chafetz 1984:118) nor young men, old ones (Irons 1983:208). Human dominance derives from talents like competence, nurturance, flattery, and deception (Maccoby and Jacklin 1974:274).

Thus, as the constraints of lactation diminished during the twentieth century owing to the decline in fertility and the increasing use of bottle feeding, women came to enter both the political and military arenas. In principle, women could attain the highest political offices, and in practice, they increasingly have done so. This tendency is less marked in military organizations. Twentieth-century warfare deeply affected the position of women but neither in principle nor practice could women attain the highest positions (Browning 2002:137–9). Their participation typically has been limited to the plethora of "female" occupations needed to conduct modern wars.[5]

In World War I, the British eventually allowed women to join the army but only in a volunteer corps limited to noncombat duties such as typing and cooking. The French used civilians for such tasks. In Russia, so many women joined frontline troops disguised as men that women were asked to form their own units after the February Revolution. Most of the combatant states gave women the right to vote, except France, where they could not vote until after World War II.

Changes that had been made during World War I were more easily accepted in World War II (Browning 2002:172–6). The relatively modest pressures of war on the United States reinforced traditional family values. By contrast, in the United Kingdom and the Soviet Union both men and women fought for national survival. Soviet women fought on a scale never seen before, though the British refused to let the women join the Home Guard, formed in 1940 as a potential partisan force in event of invasion. The demands of war eventually became so great that the British government had to require women to do war work. The Nazis, demonstrating the triumph of ideology over common sense, kept women at home. They reversed this policy late in the war but by then it didn't matter.

Combat Service and Gender Equality

Some authors, including both pro- and antifeminists, hold that experience in combat is the sine qua non of gender equality. Profeminists argue that only combat service can entitle women to the most significant social rewards. Antifeminists argue that letting women engage in combat will seriously weaken a nation's military forces.

Both sides tend to agree that the bonds men form in combat create a masculine mystique that excludes women. Men's ability to defend their group is rewarded with the highest honors. On a more prosaic level, emperors and kings in the past and elected legislators today typically give special privileges to those who have so served. A significant example is the so-called GI Bill of Rights after World War II that enabled disproportionate numbers of males to become college graduates and left disproportionate numbers of females less prepared to enter the postwar labor market. Exclusion from combat has limited women's access to education, job training, preferences in state and federal employment, retirement benefits, medical care, low-cost insurance, bonuses, and loans (Peach 1996:175). Such goodies smooth the way to success in public and private arenas, and serve as indicators that service in combat has outranked the rearing of children in its importance to national interests.

Once upon a time I too believed that service in combat was the key to gender equality. I was reared in a household influenced by Mennonite and Quaker beliefs about military service, but the failure of the "civilized" nations to contain Hitler in the 1930s convinced me that Bertrand Russell had correctly claimed that pacifism abandons the weak to the predatory. During World War II, as many friends in military service worked in unpleasant and dangerous places while I amassed social capital on a pleasant university campus, I concluded that women should be drafted for full service. How can you claim a right to equality when you let others fight your battles?

Battles may be fought for as long as our species dominates the planet, but technology has so increased the probability of irreversible catastrophe through the use of nuclear weapons that the total war may become a thing of the past lest we all go together when we go. Some military analysts hold that total mobilization in dominant states will not occur again because dominant nations can engage only in restricted wars with limited numbers of personnel (see van Crefeld 1993, Chapter 1). Others disagree. I do not know.

The Importance of Politics

It seems only fair that women serve in the same range of military occupations as men do and incur the same costs and benefits, but it seems unlikely that gender inequality hinges on such service. The gendering of institutions will far more likely erode as women increase their participation in the making and enforcing of the rules. Legal change can go far to ensure that both sexes may compete fully in the activities that bring the highest rewards. The law may not immediately change what people believe, but it can induce fairly rapid behavioral change, as demonstrated by the effort to create a nonracist military force in America (Moskos and Butler 1996).

The degendering of human institutions must overcome long years of custom. Gender socialization runs deep. Until about a century ago gender roles reflected the fact that no man could feed an infant the only food it could digest. The image of the nurturing female convinced some feminists that women will always play distinctive roles, but as sociologist Cynthia Epstein (1988) has said, gender distinctions can be deceptive. Women's behaviors and beliefs, like men's, reflect the costs and benefits they encounter in their daily work (Kanter 1977). Women's rising participation in politics is unlikely to result in utopia, but it will likely ensure further erosion of the barriers precluding women's entry to the full range of human affairs.

Notes

1. Rearranging the workplace to suit nursing mothers has been slow. Only six states require employers to allow time off and provide clean, private space for nursing an infant (Shellenbarger 2005:D4).

2. Herodotus claimed that Sarmatian women warriors did not marry until they had killed an enemy in battle (Barfield 1993:196). Women warriors have been reported in Albania, Amazonia, Angola, Arabia, Australia, the Canary Islands, Central America, Hawaii, Tasmania, and among Ainu and Apache (Davie 1929:30–34; Wright 1942:84).

3. I am indebted to Steven Rytina for insightful comment on this issue.

4. Eminent historian William McNeill (1995:41) reports the effect of group indoctrination that he experienced during World War II: Marching about in the hot Texas sun gave recruits a pervasive sense of well-being, of personal enlargement, a swelling out and becoming larger than life. However, Browning (2002:7) says that McNeill's claims for the benefits of close-order drill need to be reconciled with the high desertion rates.

5. Until 1972, Israeli women's combat service was seen as being unrestricted, but Israeli feminists soon reported problems. Despite a legend of heroism carefully cultivated and eagerly accepted by admirers abroad, Israeli women served at a much lower rate than did men and had limited chances for promotion (van Crefeld 2001:188).

References

Altmann, Jeanne. 1974. "Observational Study of Behavior: Sampling Methods." *Behavior* 49:227–267, cited in Fedigan and Fedigan (1989:44).

———. 1980. *Baboon Mothers and Infants*. Cambridge: Harvard University Press.

Altmann, Jeanne, R. Sapolsky, and P. Licht. 1995. "Baboon Fertility and Social Status." *Nature* 377:688–697.

Altmann, Stuart. 1998. *Foraging for Survival: Yearling Baboons in Africa*. Chicago: University of Chicago Press.

Andrewski, Stanislav. 1968. *Military Organization and Society*. Berkeley: University of California Press.

Asch, Beth, and James Hosek. 2004. "Breaking Ranks: U.S. Commanders Need Flexible Ways to Manage Personnel." *Rand Review* 28 (Fall).

Barfield, Thomas. 1993. *The Nomadic Alternative*. Englewood Cliffs, NJ: Prentice-Hall.

Barnes, Kathleen, George Armelagos, and Steven Morreale. 1999. "Darwinian Medicine and the Emergence of Allergy." In *Evolutionary Medicine*, Wenda Trevathan, E. O. Smith, and James McKenna, eds. New York: Oxford University Press.

Beck, Benjamin, Tara Stoinski, Michael Hutchins, Terry Maple, Bryan Norton, Andrew Rowan, Elizabeth Stevens, and Arnold Luke, eds. 2001. *Great Apes and Humans: The Ethics of Coexistence*. Washington, DC: Smithsonian.

Bentley, Gilliam. 1996. "Reconstructing Fertility from the Archeological Record." In *Gender and Archeology*, Rita Wright, ed. Philadelphia: University of Pennsylvania Press.

Berger, Peter, and Thomas Luckman. 1966. *The Social Construction of Reality*. Garden City, NJ: Doubleday.

Binford, Lewis. 1989. *Debating Archeology*. New York: Academic.
Birdsell, J. B. 1975. *Human Evolution*. Chicago: Rand McNally.
Blum, Linda. 1999. *Ideologies of Breastfeeding in the Contemporary United States*. Boston: Beacon.
Blumberg, Rae Lesser. 1978. *Stratification*. Dubuque, IA: Brown.
———. 1984. "A General Theory of Gender Stratification." *Sociological Theory 1984*. San Francisco: Jossey-Bass.
Blumberg, Rae Lesser, ed. 1995. *Engendering Wealth and Well-being*. Boulder: Westview.
Bohannon, Paul, ed. 1967. *Law and Warfare*. Garden City, NJ: Natural History Press.
Boserup, Ester. 1965. *The Conditions of Agricultural Growth*. Chicago: Aldine.
Boswell, John. 1988. *The Kindness of Strangers: The Abandonment of Children from Late Antiquity to the Renaissance*. Harmondsworth, UK: Penguin.
Bourliere, Francois. 1961. "Patterns of Social Grouping in Primates." In *The Social Life of Early Man*, Sherwood Washburn, ed. Chicago: Aldine.
Braudel, Fernand. 1979. *The Structures of Everyday Life*, Sian Reynolds, trans. and ed. New York: Harper and Row.
Brown, Judith. 1970. "A Note on the Division of Labor by Sex." *American Anthropologist* 72:1073–1078.
Browning, Peter. 2002. *The Development of Land Warfare from 1792 to 1945*. New York: Cambridge University Press.
Buss, David. 1996. "Evolutionary Insights into Feminism." In *Sex, Power, and Conflict*, David Buss and Neil Malamuth, eds. New York: Oxford University Press.
Butynski, Thomas. 2001. "Africa's Great Apes." In *Great Apes and Humans: The Ethics of Coexistence*, Beck et al., eds. Washington, DC: Smithsonian.
Butz, William. 1977. "Economic Aspects of Breast-feeding." In *Nutrition and Human Reproduction*, Henry Mosely, ed. New York: Plenum.
Caldwell, Pat, and John Caldwell. 1981. "Causes and Consequences of the Reduction in Postnatal Abstinence in Ibadan City, Nigeria." In *Child-spacing in Tropical Africa*, Hilary Page and Ron Lesthaege, eds. London: Academic.
Carneiro, Robert. 1990. "Chiefdom-level War." In *The Anthology of War*, Jonathan Haas, ed. New York: Cambridge University Press.

Cavalli-Sforza, Luigi Luca. 2000. *Genes, Peoples, and Languages,* Mark Seielsted, trans. New York: North Point Press.

Cavalli-Sforza, Luigi Luca, and Francesco Cavalli-Sforza. 1995. *The Great Diaspora,* Sarah Throne, trans. Reading, MA: Addison Wesley.

Cavalli-Sforza, Luigi Luca, and M. W. Feldman. 1981. *Cultural Transmission and Evolution: A Quantitative Approach.* Princeton, NJ: Princeton University Press.

Cavalli-Sforza, Luigi Luca, Paolo Menozzi, and Alberto Piazza. 1994. *The History and Geography of the Human Gene.* Princeton, NJ: Princeton University Press.

Chafetz, Janet Saltzman. 1984. *Sex and Advantage.* Totowa, NJ: Rowman and Allenheld.

———. 1990. *Gender Equity.* Newbury Park, CA: Sage.

———. 1999. "Structure, Consciousness, Agency, and Social Change in Feminist Sociological Theories." *Current Perspectives in Social Theory* 19:145–164.

Childe, Gordon. 1951. *Man Makes Himself.* New York: Mentor.

Cohen, Mark. 1977. *The Food Crisis in Prehistory.* New Haven, CT: Yale University Press.

———. 1984. "Introduction." In *Paleopathology at the Origins of Agriculture,* Mark Cohen and George Armelagos, eds. New York: Academic.

———. 1989. *Health and the Rise of Civilization.* New Haven, CT: Yale University Press.

Collins, Randall. 1998. *The Sociology of Philosophies.* Cambridge, MA: Belknap.

Collins, Randall, Janet Chafetz, Rae Blumberg, Scott Coltrane, and Jonathan Turner. 1993. "Toward an Integrated Theory of Gender Stratification." *Sociological Perspectives* 36:185–216.

Conkey, Margaret, and Joan Gero. 1997. "Gender and Feminism in Anthropology." *Annual Review of Anthropology* 26:411–447.

Crenshaw, Edward, and Kristopher Robison. 2005. "The Sociodemographic Roots of Economic Growth." Unpublished paper, Ohio State.

Crews, Douglas. 2003. *Human Senescence.* New York: Cambridge University Press.

Crews, Douglas, and Gary James. 1991. "Human Evolution and Genetic Epidemiology of Chronic Degenerative Diseases." In *Biological Anthropology and Human Affairs,* C. G. Mascie-Taylor and G. W. Lasker, eds. New York: Cambridge University Press.

Crews, Douglas, and L. M. Gerger. 1994. "Chronic Degenerative Diseases and Agriculture." In *Biological Anthropology and Agriculture,* Douglas Crews and R. M. Garruto, eds. New York: Oxford University Press.

Cronin, Helena. 1991. *The Ant and the Peacock: Altruism and Sexual Selection from Darwin to Today.* New York: Cambridge University Press.

Darwin, Charles. 1936 [1859]. *The Origin of Species.* New York: Modern Library, cited in Fedigan 1986.

Da Vanzo, Julie. 1988. "Infant Mortality and Socio-economic Development." *Demography* 25:581–595.

Davie, Maurice. 1929. *The Evolution of War.* New Haven, CT: Yale University Press.

Davis, Kingley, and Judith Blake. 1956. "Social Structure and Fertility." *Economic Development and Cultural Change* 4:211–235.

Dawkins, Richard. 1976. *The Selfish Gene.* New York: Oxford University Press.

De Beauvoir, Simone. 1957. *The Second Sex,* H. M. Parshley, trans. and ed. New York: Knopf.

Degler, Carl. 1991. *In Search of Human Nature.* New York: Oxford University Press.

DeVore, Irven. 1965. "Preface." In *Primate Societies,* Irven DeVore, ed. New York: Holt, Rinehart, and Winston.

DeVore, Irven, and Sherwood Washburn. 1963. "Baboon Ecology and Human Evolution." In *African Ecology and Human Evolution,* Frank Howell and Francois Bourliere, eds. Chicago: Aldine.

De Waal, Frans. 1982. *Chimpanzee Politics: Power and Sex among Apes.* New York: Harper and Row.

———. 2001a. "Introduction." In *Tree of Origin,* Frans de Waal, ed. Cambridge, MA: Harvard University Press.

———. 2001b. "Apes from Venus: Bonobos and Human Social Evolution." In *Tree of Origin,* Frans de Waal, ed. Cambridge, MA: Harvard University Press.

Diamond, Jared. 1992. *The Third Chimpanzee.* New York: HarperCollins.

———. 1997. *Guns, Germs, and Steel.* New York: W. W. Norton.

———. 2002. "Darwin's Cathedral: Evolution, Religion, and the Nature of Society." *New York Review of Books* XLIX:17.

———. 2005. *Collapse.* New York: Viking Penguin.

Di Leonardo, Micaela, ed. 1991. *Gender at the Crossroads: Feminist Anthropology in Historical Perspective.* Berkeley: University of California Press.

———. 1998. *Exotics at Home.* Chicago: University of Chicago Press.

Dos Guimaraes Sa, Isabel. 2000. "Circulation of Children in Eighteenth Century Portugal." In *Abandoned Children,* Catherine Panter-Brick and Malcolm Smith, eds. New York: Cambridge University Press.

Doyle, Michael. 1997. *Ways of War and Peace.* New York: W. W. Norton.

Dunbar, Robin. 1996. *Gossip, Grooming, and the Evolution of Language.* Cambridge, MA: Harvard University Press.

Dupuy, Trevor. 1980. *Evolution of Weapons and Warfare.* Indianapolis: Bobbs-Merrill.

Dyson-Hudson, Rada, and Neville Dyson-Hudson. 1980. "Nomadic Pastoralists." *Annual Review of Anthropology* 9:15–61.

Earle, Timothy. 1997. *How Chiefs Come to Power.* Palo Alto, CA: Stanford University Press.

Eaton, Boyd, S. B. Eaton III, and Melvin Konner. "Paleolithic Nutrition Revisited." In *Evolutionary Medicine,* Wenda Trevathan, E. O. Smith, and James McKenna, eds. New York: Oxford University Press.

Eberhard, William. 1996. *Sexual Selection by Cryptic Female Choice.* Princeton, NJ: Princeton University Press.

Ehrenberg, Margaret. 1989. *Women in Prehistory.* London: British Museum Publications.

Eibl-Eibesfeldt, Irenaeus. 1979. *The Biology of Peace and War.* New York: Viking.

Eller, Cynthia. 2000. *The Myth of Patriarchal Prehistory.* Boston: Beacon.

Ellison, Peter. 1994. "Advances in Human Reproductive Ecology." *Annual Review of Anthropology* 23:255–275.

———. 1995. "Breastfeeding, Fertility, and Maternal Condition." In *Breastfeeding,* Patricia Stuart-Macadam and Katherine Dettwyler, eds. New York: Aldine de Gruyter.

———. 1999. "Reproductive Ecology and Reproductive Cancers." In *Hormones, Health, and Behavior,* Catherine Panter-Brick and Carol Worthman, eds. New York: Cambridge University Press.

El Saadawi, Nawal. 1982. *The Hidden Face of Eve: Women in the Arab World.* Boston: Beacon.

Elshtain, Jean. 1987. *Women and War.* New York: BasicBooks.

Ember, Carol, and Melvin Ember. 1992. "Resource Unpredictability, Mistrust, and War." *Journal of Conflict Resolution* 36:242–262.

Enloe, Cynthia. 1993. *The Morning After.* Berkeley: University of California Press.

Epstein, Cynthia. 1988. *Deceptive Distinctions: Sex, Gender, and the Social Order.* New Haven, CT: Yale University Press.

Falk, Dean. 1992. "Brain Evolution and Hominid Cognition." The 62nd Arthur Lecture, New York. The American Museum of Natural History. Cited in Falk 1997.

———. 1997. "Brain Evolution in Females: An Answer to Mr. Lovejoy." In *Women in Evolution,* Lori Hager, ed. London: Routledge.

Fedigan, Linda. 1992 [1982]. *Primate Paradigms.* Chicago: University of Chicago Press.

———. 1986. "Women's Changing Role in Models of Evolution." *Annual Review of Anthropology* 18:245–266.

Fedigan, Linda, and Larry Fedigan. 1989. "Gender and the Study of Primates." In *Gender and Anthropology,* Sandra Morgen, ed. Washington, DC: American Anthropological Association.

Fildes, Valerie. 1986. *Breasts, Bottles, and Babies.* Edinburgh: Edinburgh University Press.

———. 1988. *Wet Nursing: A History from Antiquity to the Present.* Oxford, UK: Blackwell.

Flax, Jane. 1987. "Postmodernism and Gender Relations in Feminist Theory." *SIGNS* 12:621–643.

Flinn, Mark. 1999. "Family Environment, Stress, and Health." In *Hormones, Health, and Behavior,* C. Panter-Brick and C. M. Worthman, eds. New York: Cambridge University Press.

Fried, Morton. 1967. *The Evolution of Political Society.* New York: Random House.

———. 1978. "The State, the Chicken, and the Egg." In *Origins of the State,* Ronald Cohen and Elman Service, eds. Philadelphia: Institute for the Study of Human Issues.

Friedan, Betty. 1963. *The Feminine Mystique.* New York: W. W. Norton.

Friedl, Ernestine. 1975. *Women and Men: An Anthropologist's View.* New York: Holt, Rinehart, and Winston.

Galloway, Alison. 1997. "The Cost of Reproduction and the Evolution of Post-Menopausal Osteoporosis." In *The Evolving Female,* Mary Ellen Morbeck, Alison Galloway, and Adrienne Zihlman, eds. Princeton, NJ: Princeton University Press.

Garden, Maurice. 1975. *Lyon et les Lyonnais au XVIIIe Siècle.* Paris: Flammarion.

Gioiosa, R. 1955. "Incidence of Pregnancy during Lactation in 500 Cases." *American Journal of Obstetrics and Gynecology* 70:162–174. Cited in Ellison 1995.

Golden, Janet. 2001. *A Social History of Wet Nursing in America.* Columbus: Ohio State University Press.

Goldman, Nancy. 1973. "Women's Changing Role in the Armed Forces." In *Changing Women in a Changing Society,* Joan Huber, ed. Chicago: University of Chicago Press.

Goodall, Jane. 1965. "New Discoveries among Africa's Chimpanzees." *National Geographic* 128:802–831, cited in Washburn 1968.

Goody, Jack. 1962. *Death, Property, and the Ancestors.* Palo Alto, CA: Stanford University Press.

———. 1971. *Technology, Tradition, and the State.* London: Oxford University Press.

———. 1976. *Production and Reproduction.* Cambridge, UK: Cambridge University Press.

———. 1983. *The Development of the Family and Marriage in Europe.* Cambridge, UK: Cambridge University Press.

Goody, Jack, and Stanley Tambiah. 1973. *Bridewealth and Dowry.* Cambridge, UK: Cambridge University Press.

Gould, Stephen. 1983. *Hen's Teeth and Horse's Toes.* New York: W. W. Norton.

———. 1996. *Full House.* New York: Harmony.

Gowaty, Patricia, ed. 1997. *Feminism and Evolutionary Biology.* New York: Chapman and Hall.

Granovetter, Mark. 1979. "The Idea of 'Advancement' in Theories of Evolution and Development." *American Journal of Sociology* 85:489–515.

Gray, Sandra. 1999. "Infant Care and Feeding." In *Turkana Herders of the Dry Savanna,* Michael Little and Paul Leslie, eds. New York: Oxford University Press.

Greenberg, Joseph. 2005. *Genetic Linguistics,* William Croft, ed., with introduction and bibliography. New York: Oxford University Press.

Haaga, John. 1988. "Reliability of Retrospective Survey Data." *Demography* 25:307–314.

———. 1993. "Behavioral Biology and the Study of Human Fertility: A Review Essay." *Population and Development Review* 29:505–517.

Hamilton, Richard. 1999. "Problematic Sociology Textbooks on War and the Military." Unpublished paper, Ohio State.

Haraway Donna. 1989. *Primate Visions.* New York: Routledge.

Harris, Marvin. 1969. *The Rise of Anthropological Theory.* New York: Crowell.

Hastrup, Kirsten. 1985. *Medieval Iceland.* Oxford, UK: Clarendon.

Heather, Peter. 1996. *The Goths.* Cambridge, UK: Blackwell.

Hechter, Michael. 1987. *Principles of Group Solidarity.* Berkeley: University of California Press.

Heider, Karl. 1972. "Environment, Subsistence, and Society." *Annual Review of Anthropology* 1:207–226.

Henry, Louis. 1953. *Fecondité de marriages, nouvelle methode de mesure.* Paris: Presses Universitaire de France.

———. 1961. "Some Data on Natural Fertility." *Eugenics Quarterly* 8:81–91.

Herskovitz, Melville. 1938. *Dahomey II.* New York: Augustin and Northwestern University Press.

Hervada, A. R., and D. R. Newman. 1992. "Weaning." *Current Problems in Pediatrics* 22: 223. Cited in Lawrence and Lawrence, 1999:336.

Hill, Kim, and Magdalena Hurtado. 1996. *Ache Life History: The Ecology and Demography of a Foraging People.* New York: Aldine de Gruyter.

Hobcraft, John. 1994. "Why Can't Demographers and Physiologists Agree?" In *Human Reproductive Ecology,* Kenneth Campbell and James Wood, eds. New York: New York Academy of Science.

———. 2003. "Reflections on Demographic, Evolutionary, and Genetic Approaches to Human Reproductive Behavior." In *Offspring: Human Fertility Behavior in Biodemographic Perspective,* Kenneth Wachter and Rudolfo Bulatao, eds. Washington, DC: National Academies Press.

Hobhouse, L. T., G. C. Wheeler, and M. Ginsberg. 1930. *Material Culture and Social Institutions of the Simpler Peoples.* London: Routledge and Kegan Paul.

Holm, Jeanne. 1982. *Women in the Military.* Novato, CA: Presidio.

Hosken, Fran. 1979. *Genital and Sexual Mutilation of Females.* Lexington: Women's International Network News.

Howell, Nancy. 1979. *Demography of the Dobe !Kung.* New York: Academic.

Hrdy, Sarah Blaffer. 1979. "Infanticide among Animals: Implications for Female Reproductive Strategies." *Ethology and Sociobiology* 1:13–40.

———. 1981. *The Woman Who Never Evolved.* Cambridge, MA: Harvard University Press.

———. 1990. "Sex Bias in Nature and History: A Late 1980s Reexamination of the 'Biological Origins' Argument." *Yearbook of Physical Anthropology* 33:25–37.

———. 1999. *Mother Nature: A History of Mothers, Infants, and Natural Selection.* New York: Pantheon.

Hrdy, Sarah, and George Williams. 1983. "Behavioral Biology and the Double Standard." In *Social Behavior of Female Vertebrates,* Samuel Wasser, ed. New York: Academic.

Huber, Joan. 1976. "Toward a Socio-technological Theory of the Women's Movement." *Social Problems* 23:371–383.

———. 1990. "Macro-micro Links in Gender Stratification." *American Sociological Review* 55:1–10.

———. 1999. "Comparative Gender Stratification." In *The Handbook of Gender Sociology,* Janet Saltzman Chafetz, ed. New York: Plenum.

———. 2004. "Lenski Effects on Social Stratification Theory." *Sociological Theory* 22:258–268.

Huber, Joan, and Glenna Spitze. 1981. "Wives' Employment, Household Behaviors, and Sex-Role Attitudes." *Social Forces* 60:150–169.

———. 1983. *Sex Stratification: Children, Housework, and Jobs.* New York: Academic.

Ingold, Timothy. 1986. *Evolution and Social Life.* Cambridge, UK: Cambridge University Press.

Jablonski, Nina. 2004. "The Evolution of Human Skin and Skin Color." *Annual Review of Anthropology* 33:585–623.

Jackman, Mary. 1994. *The Velvet Glove.* Berkeley: University of California Press.

Jackson, Robert Max. 1998. *Destined for Equality.* Cambridge, MA: Harvard University Press.

Janowitz, Morris. 1960. *The Professional Soldier.* Glencoe, IL: Free Press.

———. 1971. *The Professional Soldier.* New York: Free Press.

Janson, Charles. 1992. "Evolutionary Ecology of Primate Social Structure." In *Evolutionary Ecology and Human Behavior,* Eric Alden Smith and Bruce Winterhalder, eds. New York: Aldine de Gruyter.

Jelliffe, Derrick, and Patricia Jelliffe. 1978. "Volume and Composition of Milk in Poorly Nourished Communities." *American Journal of Clinical Nutrition* 31:492–515.

Jenkins, Craig, and William Form. 2005. "Social Movements and Social Change." In *The Handbook of Political Sociology,* Thomas Janowski, Robert Alford, Alexander Hicks, and Mildred Schwartz, eds. Cambridge, UK: Cambridge University Press.

Johnson, Allen, and Timothy Earle. 1987. *The Evolution of Human Societies.* Palo Alto, CA: Stanford University Press.

Jolly, Alison. 1999. *Lucy's Legacy.* Cambridge, MA: Harvard University Press.

Kano, Takayoshi, and Evelyn Ono Vineberg. 1992. *The Last Ape: Pygmy Chimpanzee Behavior and Ecology.* Palo Alto, CA: Stanford University Press.

Kanter, Rosabeth Moss. 1977. *Men and Women of the Corporation.* New York: BasicBooks.

Kaplan, Hillard, and Jane Lancaster. 2003. "An Evolutionary and Ecological Analysis of Human Fertility, Mating Patterns, and Parental Investment." In *Offspring: Human Behavior in Biodemographic Perspective,* Kenneth Wachter and Rudolfo Bulatao, eds. Washington, DC: National Academies Press.

Kaplan, H. S., K. Hill, A. M. Hurtado, and J. B. Lancaster. 2001. "The Embodied Capital Theory of Human Evolution." In *Reproductive Ecology and Human Evolution,* P. T. Ellison, ed. New York: Aldine de Gruyter.

Keegan, John. *The Mask of Command.* New York: Penguin.

———. 1996. *The Battle for History: Re-fighting World War II.* New York: Vintage.

Keeley, Lawrence. 1996. *War before Civilization.* New York: Oxford University Press.

Kelly, Robert. 1995. *The Foraging Spectrum.* Washington, DC: Smithsonian.

Kelso, A. J., and Wenda Trevathan. 1984. *Physical Anthropology,* 3rd ed. Englewood Cliffs, NJ: Prentice-Hall.

Kerber, Linda. 1998. *No Constitutional Right to Be Ladies.* New York: Hill and Wang.

Kertzer, David. 1993. *Sacrificed for Honor.* Boston: Beacon.

Kirk, Dudley. 1968. "The Field of Demography." In *International Encyclopedia of the Social Sciences,* vol. 12, David Sills, ed. New York: Macmillan/Free Press.

Knodel, John. 1988. *Demographic Behavior in the Past.* Cambridge, UK: Cambridge University Press.

Komaroff, Anthony, ed. 1999. *The Harvard Medical School Family Health Guide.* New York: Simon and Schuster.
Konner, Melvin. 1982. *The Tangled Wing.* New York: Holt, Rinehart, and Winston.
Lancaster, Jane. 1975. *Primate Behavior and the Emergence of Human Culture.* New York: Holt, Rinehart, and Winston.
———. 1985. "Evolutionary Perspectives on Sex Differences in the Higher Primates." In *Gender and the Life Course,* Alice Rossi, ed. New York: Aldine de Gruyter.
———. 1991. "A Feminist and Evolutionary Biologist Looks at Women." *Yearbook of Physical Anthropology* 34:1–11.
Lancaster, Jane, and Chet Lancaster. 1983. "Parental Investment: The Hominid Adaptation." In *How Humans Adapt,* Donald Ortner, ed. Washington, DC: Smithsonian.
Larsen, Clark. 2000. *Skeletons in Our Closet.* Princeton, NJ: Princeton University Press.
Lawrence, Ruth, and Robert Lawrence. 1994. *Breastfeeding,* 4th ed. St. Louis, MO: Mosby.
———. 1999. *Breastfeeding,* 5th ed. St. Louis, MO: Mosby.
LeBlanc, Steven. 1999. *Prehistoric War in the American Southwest.* Salt Lake City: University of Utah Press.
Lee, P. C. 1996. "Fertility Constraints in Non-human Mammals." In *Variability in Human Fertility,* Lyliane Rosetta and C. G. N. Mascie-Taylor, eds. Cambridge, UK: Cambridge University Press.
Lee, Richard, and Irven DeVore. 1968. "Preface." In *Man the Hunter,* Richard Lee and Irven DeVore, eds. Chicago: Aldine-Atherton.
Lee, Richard, and Irven DeVore, eds. *Kalahari Hunter-Gatherers.* Cambridge, MA: Harvard University Press.
Lehrer, Tom. 1986. *Tom Foolery,* Cameron Mackintosh and Robin Ray, adapters. New York: French.
Lenski, Gerhard. 1966. *Power and Privilege.* New York: McGraw-Hill.
———. 1970. *Human Societies.* New York: McGraw-Hill.
———. 2005. *Ecological-Evolutionary Theory.* Boulder: Paradigm.
Lenski, Gerhard, and Jean Lenski. 1978. *Human Societies,* 3rd ed. New York: McGraw-Hill.
Leridon, Henry. *Human Fertility.* Chicago: University of Chicago Press.
Leutenegger, Walter. 1982. "Encephalization and Obstetrics in Primates and Human Evolution." In *Primate Brain Evolution,* Este Armstrong and Dean Falk, eds. New York: Plenum.

Levine, Robert, and Donald Campbell. 1972. *Ethnocentrism.* New York: Wiley.

Levy, Howard. 1966. *Chinese Footbinding.* New York: Walton Rawls.

Lewis, Bernard. 1997. *The Middle East.* London: Phoenix.

Lieberman, Leonard. 1989. "A Discipline Divided." *Current Anthropology* 30:676–682.

Lieberman, Philip. 1998. *Eve Spoke: Human Language and Human Evolution.* New York: W. W. Norton.

Linton, Sally. 1971. "Woman the Gatherer." In *Women in Cross-Cultural Perspective,* Sue-Ellen Jacobs, ed. Urbana-Champaign: University of Illinois Press.

Lipset, Seymour Martin. 1990. *Continental Divide.* New York: Routledge.

Little, Michael, and Paul Leslie. 1999. *Turkana Herders of the Dry Savanna.* New York: Oxford University Press.

Lopreato, Joseph, and Timothy Crippen. 1999. *Crisis in Sociology.* New Brunswick, NJ: Transaction.

Lorenz, Konrad. 1966. *On Aggression,* Marjorie Wilson, trans. New York: Harcourt, Brace, Jovanovich.

Lovejoy, C. O. 1981. "The Origin of Man." *Science* 211:341–350.

Low, Bobbi, Alice Clarke, and Kenneth Lockridge. 1992. "Toward an Ecological Demography." *Population and Development Review* 18:1–31.

Lumsden, Charles, and E. O. Wilson. 1978. "Introduction." In *Sociobiology and Human Nature,* Michael Gregory, Anita Silves, and Diane Sutch, eds. San Francisco: Jossey-Bass.

Luttberg, Barney, Monique Borgerhoff, and Marc Mangel. 2000. "To Marry or Not." In *Adaptation and Human Behavior,* Lee Cronk, Napoleon Chagnon, and William Irons, eds. New York: Aldine de Gruyter.

Mackie, G. 1996. "Ending Footbinding and Infibulation." *American Sociological Review* 61:999–1017.

Marshall, Catherine, C. K. Ogden, and Mary Florence. 1987 [1915]. *Militarism versus Feminism,* Margaret Kamester and Jo Vellacot, eds. London: Virago.

Martin, M. K., and Barbara Voorhies. 1975. *The Female of the Species.* New York: Columbia University Press.

Maryanski, Alexandra. 1996. "Was Speech an Evolutionary Afterthought?" In *Communicating Meaning: The Evolution and Development of Language,* Boris Velichkovsky and Duane Rumbaugh, eds. Mahwah, NJ: Erlbaum.

Maynard Smith, John. 1997. "Commentary." In *Feminism and Evolutionary Biology,* Patricia Gowaty, ed. New York: Chapman and Hall.

Maynard Smith, John, D. Barker, C. Finch, S. Kardia, B. Eaton, T. Kirkwood, E. LeGrand, R. Nesse, G. Williams, and L. Partridge. 1999. "The Evolution of Non-Infectious and Degenerative Disease." In *Evolution in Health and Disease,* Stephen Stearns, ed. New York: Oxford University Press.

Mayr, Ernest. 1982. *The Growth of Biological Thought.* Cambridge, MA: Belknap.

———. 1978. "The Nature of the Darwinian Revolution." In *Human Evolution: Biosocial Perspectives,* S. L. Washburn and Elizabeth McCown, eds. Menlo Park, CA: Benjamin Cummings.

———. 1997. *This Is Biology.* Cambridge, MA: Belknap.

Mazur, Allan, and Alan Booth. 1998. "Testosterone and Dominance in Men." *Behavioral and Brain Sciences* 21:353–363.

McGrew, William. 2001. "The Nature of Culture." In *Tree of Origin,* Frans de Waal, ed. Cambridge, MA: Harvard University Press.

McKeown, Thomas. 1976. *The Role of Medicine.* London: Provincial Hospitals Trust.

McNeill, William. 1982. *The Pursuit of Power.* Chicago: University of Chicago Press.

———. 1995. *Keeping Together in Time.* Cambridge, MA: Harvard University Press.

McNeilly, A. W. 1993. "Breast-feeding and Fertility." In *Biomedical and Demographic Determinants of Reproduction,* Ronald Gray, ed., with Henry Leridon and Alfred Spira. Oxford, UK: Clarendon.

Mealey, Linda. 2000. *Sex Differences.* San Diego, CA: Academic.

Micozzi, Marc. 1995. "Breast Cancer and Breastfeeding." In *Breastfeeding,* Patricia Stuart-Macadam and Katherine Dettwyler, eds. New York: Aldine de Gruyter.

Mittermeier, Russell, and Dorothy Cheney. 1987. "Conservation of Primates and Their Habitats." In *Primate Societies,* Barbara Smuts, Dorothy Cheney, Robert Seyfarth, Richard Wrangham, and Thomas Struhsaker, eds. Chicago: University of Chicago Press.

Money, John. 1995. *Gendermaps.* New York: Continuum.

Moon, Katherine. 1997. *Sex among Allies: Military Prostitution in U.S.-Korea Relations.* New York: Columbia University Press.

Morris, Desmond. 1967. *The Naked Ape.* New York: McGraw-Hill.

Moseley, K. P., and I. Wallerstein. 1978. "Precapitalist Social Structures." *Annual Review of Anthropology* 4:259–290.

Moskos, Charles. 1971. "The Emergent Military." In *Public Opinion and the Military Establishment,* Charles Moskos, ed. Beverly Hills, CA: Sage.

———. 2000. "Toward a Postmodern Military: The United States." In *The Postmodern Military,* Charles Moskos, John A. Williams, and John Sibley Butler, eds. New York: Oxford University Press.

Mukhopadhyay, Carol, and Patricia Higgins. 1988. "Anthropological Studies of Women's Status Revisited." *Annual Review of Anthropology* 17:461–495.

Napier, J. 1993 [1967]. "The Antiquity of Walking." In *Human Evolution Source Book,* Russell Ciochon and John Fleagle, eds. Englewood Cliffs, NJ: Prentice-Hall.

Nesse, Randolph, and George Williams. 1994. *Why We Get Sick.* New York: Vintage.

Netting, Robert. 1993. *Smallholders, Householders.* Palo Alto, CA: Stanford University Press.

Otterbein, Keith. 1999. "A History of Research on Warfare in Anthropology." *American Anthropologist* 101:794–805.

Page, Hilary, and Ron Lesthaege. 1981. "Preface." In *Child-spacing in Tropical Africa,* Hilary Page and Ron Lesthaege, eds. London: Academic.

Palloni, Alberto, and Marta Tienda. 1986. "Effects of Breastfeeding and Pace of Childbearing on Early Age Mortality." *Demography* 23:31–52.

Panter-Brick, Catherine. 1992a. "Working Mothers in Rural Nepal." In *The Anthropology of Breast-feeding,* Vanessa Maher, ed. Oxford, UK: Berg.

———. 1992b. "Women's Working Behavior and Maternal-Child Health in Rural Nepal." In *Physical Activity and Health,* N. G. Norgan, ed. Cambridge, UK: Cambridge University Press.

Peach, Lucinda. 1996. "Gender Ideology in the Ethics of Combat." In *It's Our Military Too,* Judith Stiehm, ed. Philadelphia, PA: Temple University Press.

Pfeiffer, John. 1978. *The Emergence of Man,* 3rd ed. New York: Harper and Row.

Potts, Malcolm, and Roger Short. 1999. *Ever Since Adam and Eve: The Evolution of Human Sexuality.* Cambridge, UK: Cambridge University Press.

Potts, Rick. 1996. *Humanity's Descent.* New York: William Morrow.

Preston, Samuel, and Michael Haines. 1991. *Fatal Years.* Princeton, NJ: Princeton University Press.

Pusey, Anne. 2001. "Chimpanzee Social Organization and Reproduction." In *Tree of Origin,* Frans de Waal, ed. Cambridge, MA: Harvard University Press.

Quandt, Sara. 1995. "Sociocultural Aspects of Lactation." In *Breastfeeding,* Patricia Stuart-Macadam and Katherine Dettwyler, eds. New York: Aldine de Gruyter.

Quinn, Naomi. 1977. "Anthropological Studies of Women's Status." *Annual Review of Anthropology* 6:181–225.

Ransel, David. 1988. *Mothers of Misery.* Princeton, NJ: Princeton University Press.

Rodriguez, German, and Soledad Diaz. 1993. "Breastfeeding and the Length of Post-Partum Amenorrhea." In *Biomedical and Demographic Determinants of Reproduction,* Henri Leridon and Jane Menken, eds. Oxford, UK: Clarendon.

Rosaldo, Michelle. 1980. "The Use and Abuse of Anthropology." *SIGNS* 5:389–417.

Rossi, Alice. 1983. "Gender and Parenthood." *American Sociological Review* 49:1–19.

———. "Eros and Caritas: A Biopsychosocial Approach to Human Sexuality and Reproduction." In *Sexuality across the Life Course,* Alice Rossi, ed. Chicago: University of Chicago Press.

Rothman, Barbara Katz, ed. 1993. *Encyclopedia of Childbearing.* Phoenix, AZ: Oryx.

Rovee-Collier, Caroline, and Lewis Lipsitt. 1982. "Learning, Adaptation, and Memory in the Newborn." In *Psychobiology of the Human Newborn,* Peter Stratton, ed. New York: John Wiley.

Rowell, Thelma. 1972. *The Social Behavior of Monkeys.* New York: Penguin.

———. 1999. "The Myth of Peculiar Primates." In *Mammalian Social Learning,* Hilary Box and Kathleen Gibson, eds. Cambridge, UK: Cambridge University Press.

Ruhlen, Merritt. 1987. *A Guide to the World's Languages: 1. Classification.* Palo Alto, CA: Stanford University Press.

Rule, James. 1997. *Theory and Progress in Social Science.* Cambridge, UK: Cambridge University Press.

Ruvulo, M. 1997. "Genetic Diversity in Hominoid Primates." *Annual Review of Anthropology* 26:515–540.

Rytina, Steven. 2000. "Social Structure." In *Encyclopedia of Sociology,* 2nd ed., Edgar Borgatta, ed. New York: Macmillan.

———. 2001. Personal communication.

Sanday, Peggy. 1973. "Toward a Theory of the Status of Women." *American Anthropologist* 75:1682–1700.

Savage-Rumbaugh, Sue Stuart Shanker, and Talbot Taylor. 1998. *Apes, Language, and Mind.* New York: Oxford University Press.

Scheper-Hughes, Nancy. 1992. *Death without Weeping.* Berkeley: University of California Press.

Scheper-Hughes, Nancy, and Carolyn Sargent. 1998. "Introduction." In *Small Wars,* Nancy Scheper-Hughes and Carolyn Sargent, eds. Berkeley: University of California Press.

Scheppele, Kim. "Legal Theory." *Annual Review of Anthropology* 20:383–406.

Schlegel, Alice. 1990. "Gender Meanings." In *Beyond the Second Sex,* Peggy Sanday, ed. Philadelphia: University of Pennsylvania Press.

Searle, John. 1995. *The Construction of Social Reality.* New York: Free Press.

Segerstrale, Ullica. 2000. *Defenders of the Truth.* Oxford: Oxford University Press.

Shellenbarger, Sue. 2005. "Work and Family Mailbox." *Wall Street Journal* CCXLV 48:D4.

Shiebinger, Londa. 1999. *Has Feminism Changed Science?* Cambridge, MA: Harvard University Press.

Shipton, Parker. 1994. "Land and Culture in Tropical Africa." *Annual Review of Anthropology* 23:347–77.

Small, Merideth. 1993. *Female Choice.* Ithaca, NY: Cornell University Press.

———. 1998. *Our Babies, Ourselves.* New York: Doubleday-Anchor.

Smuts, Barbara. 1985. *Sex and Friendship in Baboons.* New York: Aldine de Gruyter.

———. 1995. "The Evolutionary Origins of Patriarchy." *Human Nature* 6:1–32.

———. 1996. "Male Aggression against Women: An Evolutionary Perspective." In *Sex, Power, and Conflict,* David Buss and Neil Malamuth, eds. New York: Oxford University Press.

Smuts, Barbara, Dorothy Cheney, Robert Seyfarth, Richard Wrangham, and Thomas Struhsaker, eds. 1987. *Primate Societies.* Chicago: University of Chicago Press.

Sokoloff, Natalie. 1980. *Between Money and Love.* New York: Praeger.

Stanford, Craig. 2001. "Meat-eating, Meat-sharing, and Human Evolution." In *Tree of Origin,* Frans de Waal, ed. Cambridge, MA: Harvard University Press.

Steckel, Richard, and Jerome Rose. 2002. "Patterns of Health in the Western Hemisphere." In *The Backbone of History: Health and Nutrition in the Western Hemisphere,* Richard Steckel and Roderick Floud, eds. Cambridge, UK: Cambridge University Press.

Stein, Dorothy. 1978. "Suttee as a Normative Institution." *SIGNS* 4:253–268.

Stiehm, Judith. 1989. *Arms and the Enlisted Woman.* Philadelphia, PA: Temple University Press.

Stini, William. 1885. "Growth Rates and Sexual Dimorphism: An Evolutionary Perspective on Prehistoric Diets." In *The Analysis of Prehistoric Diets,* Robert Gilbert Jr. and James Mielke, eds. Orlando, FL: Academic.

Stocking, George, Jr. 1968. *Race, Culture, and Evolution.* New York: Free Press.

Stoller, M. 1977. "The Obstetric Pelvis and Mechanism of Labor in Nonhuman Primates." *American Journal of Physical Anthropology* (supp.) 20:204–213.

Stone, Glenn, and Christian Downum. 1999. "Non-Bosrupian Ecology and Agricultural Risk." *American Anthropologist* 101:113–128.

Strier, Karen. 2001. "Beyond the Apes." In *Tree of Origin,* Frans de Waal, ed. Cambridge, MA: Harvard University Press.

Stuart-Macadam, Patricia. 1995. "Biocultural Perspectives on Breastfeeding." In *Breastfeeding,* Patricia Stuart-Macadam and Katherine Dettwyler, eds. New York: Aldine de Gruyter.

———. 1998. "Iron Deficiency Anemia." In *Sex and Gender in Pathological Perspective,* Anne Grauer and Patricia Stuart-Macadam, eds. Cambridge, UK: Cambridge University Press.

Sussman, George. 1982. *Selling Mother's Milk.* Urbana-Champaign: University of Illinois Press.

Tanner, Nancy, and Adrienne Zihlman. 1976. "Innovation and Selection in Human Origins." *SIGNS* 1:585–608.

Testart, Alain. 1988. "Major Problems in the Social Anthropology of Hunter-Gatherers." *Current Anthropology* 29:1–31.

Tiger, Lionel. 1969. *Men in Groups.* New York: Random House.

Tiger, Lionel, and Robin Fox. 1971. *The Imperial Animal.* New York: Holt, Rinehart, and Winston.

Tooby, John, and Irven DeVore. 1987. "The Reconstruction of Hominid Evolution through Strategic Modeling." In *The Evolution of Human Behavior: Primate Models,* Warren Kinzey, ed. Albany: State University of New York Press.

Trevathan, Wenda. 1987. *Human Birth: An Evolutionary Perspective.* Hawthorne, NY: Aldine de Gruyter.

———. 1999. "Evolutionary Obstetrics." In *Evolutionary Medicine,* Wenda Trevathan, E. O. Smith, and James McKenna, eds. New York: Oxford University Press.

Turner, Jonathan. 1988. *The Institutional Order.* New York: Longman.

———. 1995. *Macrodynamics: Toward a Theory on the Organization of Human Populations.* New Brunswick, NJ: Rutgers University Press.

———. 2000. *On the Origins of Human Emotions.* Palo Alto, CA: Stanford University Press.

Turner, Jonathan, and Alexandra Maryanski. 2005. *Incest: Origins of the Taboo.* Boulder, CO: Paradigm.

Turney-High, Harry. 1949. *Primitive War.* New York: Columbia University Press.

Tuttle, Russell. 2001. "Phylogenies, Fossils, and Feelings." In *Great Apes and Humans: The Ethics of Coexistence,* Benjamin Beck, et al., eds. Washington, DC: Smithsonian.

Udy, Stanley. 1973. "Cross-cultural Analysis." *Annual Review of Anthropology* 2:253–270.

Van Crefeld, Martin. 1993. *Nuclear Proliferation and the Future of Conflict.* New York: Free Press.

Van den Berghe, Pierre. 1978. *Human Family Systems: An Evolutionary View.* New York: Elsevier.

Van de Walle, Etienne, and Francine van de Walle. 1993. "Postpartum Sexual Abstinence in Tropical Africa." In *Biological and Demographic Determinants of Reproduction,* Henri Leridon and Jane Menken, eds. Oxford, UK: Clarendon.

Van Esterik, Penny. 1989. *Beyond the Breast-Bottle Controversy.* New Brunswick, NJ: Rutgers University Press.

Vayda, Andrew. 1968. "Primitive War." *International Encyclopedia of the Social Sciences,* vol. 16, David Sills, ed. New York: Macmillan/Free Press.

Velichkovsky, Boris. 1996. "Language Development at the Crossroads of Biology and Culture." In *The Evolution and Development of Language,* Boris Velichkovsky and Duane Rumbaugh, eds. Mahwah, NJ: Erlbaum.

Viazzo, Pier, Maria Bortolotto, and Andrew Zanotti. 2000. "Five Centuries of Foundling History in Florence." In *Abandoned Children,* Catherine Panter-Brick and Malcolm Smith, eds. New York: Cambridge University Press.

Vitzthum, Virginia. 1994. "Comparative Study of Breastfeeding and Its Relation to Human Reproductive Ecology." *Yearbook of Physical Anthropology* 37:307–349.

———. 1997. "Adaptation in Human Reproduction." In *The Evolving Female,* Alison Galloway, Mary Ellen Morbeck, Adrienne Zihlman, eds. Princeton, NJ: Princeton University Press.

Washburn, Sherwood. 1968. "The Study of Human Evolution." Condon Lectures. Eugene: Oregon System-Higher Education.

———. 1978. "Animal Behavior and Social Anthropology." In *Sociobiology and Human Nature,* Michael Gregory, Anita Silvers, and Diane Sutch, eds. San Francisco: Jossey-Bass.

Washburn, Sherwood, and Irven DeVore. 1961. "Social Behavior of Baboons and Early Man." In *The Social Life of Early Man,* Sherwood Washburn, ed. Chicago: Aldine.

Washburn, Sherwood, and C. S. Lancaster. 1968. "The Evolution of Hunting." In *Man the Hunter,* Richard Lee and Irven DeVore, eds. Chicago: Aldine.

Washburn, Sherwood, and David Hamburg. 1965. "Implications of Primate Research." In *Primate Behavior: Field Studies of Monkeys and Apes,* Irven DeVore, ed. New York: Holt, Rinehart, and Winston.

White, Lynn. 1962. *Medieval Technology and Social Change.* New York: Oxford University Press.

Whitten, Patricia. 1999. "Diet, Hormones, and Health." In *Hormones, Health, and Behavior,* Catherine Panter-Brick and Carol Worthman, eds. Cambridge, UK: Cambridge University Press.

Whyte, Martin. 1978. *The Status of Women in Preindustrial Societies.* Princeton, NJ: Princeton University Press.

Wiley, Andrea, and Ivy Pike. 1998. "An Alternative Method to Assess Early Mortality in Contemporary Populations." *American Journal of Physical Anthropology* 107:315–330.

Wilson, Edward. 1975. *Sociobiology.* Cambridge, MA: Harvard University Press.

———. 1996. *In Search of Nature.* Washington, DC: Island Press.

———. 1998. *Consilience.* New York: Knopf.

Wolf, Jacqueline. 2001. *Public Health and the Decline of Breastfeeding.* Columbus: Ohio State University Press.

Wolpoff, M. H. 1992. "Multiregional Evolution: The Fossil Alternative to Eden." In *The Human Evolution Source Book,* Russell Ciochon and John Fleagle, eds. Englewood Cliffs, NJ: Prentice-Hall.

Worthman, Carol. 1993. "Bio-cultural Interactions in Human Development." In *Juvenile Primates,* Michael Pereira and Lynn Fairbanks, eds. Oxford: Oxford University Press.

———. 1999a. "Epidemiology of Human Development." In *Hormones, Health and Behavior,* Catherine Panter-Brick and Carol Worthman, eds. Cambridge, UK: Cambridge University Press.

———. 1999b. "Evolutionary Perspectives on the Onset of Puberty." In *Evolutionary Medicine,* Wenda Trevathan, E. O. Smith, and James McKenna, eds. New York: Oxford University Press.

World Health Organization. 1981. *Report on the WHO Collaborative Study on Breast-feeding.* Geneva: Author.

Wrangham, Richard. 2001. "Out of the Pan, into the Fire." In *Tree of Origin,* Frans de Waal, ed. Cambridge, MA: Harvard University Press.

Wray, Joe. 1977. "Maternal Nutrition, Breastfeeding, and Infant Survival." In *Nutrition and Human Reproduction,* Henry Mosely, ed. New York: Plenum.

Wright, Quincy. 1942. *A Study of War.* Chicago: University of Chicago Press.

Zihlman, Adrienne. 1978. "Subsistence and Social Organization in Early Hominids." *SIGNS* 4:4–20.

———. 1997. "Women's Bodies, Women's Lives." In *The Evolving Female: A Life History,* Mary Ellen Morbeck, Alison Galloway, and Adrienne Zihlman, eds. Princeton, NJ: Princeton University Press.

Zihlman, Adrienne, and Nancy Tanner. 1979. "Gathering and the Hominid Adaptation." In *Female Hierarchies,* Lionel Tiger and Heather Fowler, eds. Chicago: Beresford.

Zohoori, Namvar, and Barry Popkin. 1996. "Longitudinal Analysis of Infant Feeding Practices on Post-partum Amenhorrhea." *Demography* 33:167–180.

Zuk, Marlene. 2002. *Sexual Selections.* Berkeley: University of California Press.

Index

About the Author

After more than a decade of full-time housewifery, Joan Huber returned to graduate school in sociology. After receiving a PhD at Michigan State, she taught at Notre Dame and the University of Illinois at Champaign-Urbana, and then went to Ohio State in 1984 as dean of the College of Social and Behavioral Science. In 1989 she served as president of the American Sociological Association. She retired from Ohio State in 1994 as senior vice president and provost.